AUSSIE CARS

MARQUE
PUBLISHING COMPANY

FRONT COVER: Falcon in full flight.

REAR COVER: (From Top) 1896 Shearer, 1919 Australian Six, The author's 48-215 Holden versus the 1986 Holden Commodore Calais Turbo at Sydney's Oran Park racing circuit (Photo by Brian Woodward), 1958 Ascort, 1986 Mitsubishi Magna.

ENDPAPERS: Work at the Australian Six factory, circa 1921.

AUSSIE CARS

by
Tony Davis

AUSSIE CARS was written by TONY DAVIS, based on research by TONY DAVIS and PEDR DAVIS. It was first published in 1987 by MARQUE PUBLISHING COMPANY, P.O. Box 203, Hurstville, NSW 2220.

© Copyright 1987 Marque Publishing Company.

National Library of Australia

Aussie Cars

ISBN 0 947079 01 7

Proudly produced wholly within Australia.

Typeset by Terry Clark Typesetters Pty. Ltd. (Kogarah, NSW).
Design and layout by Tony Davis/Cover by Irene Meier.
Copy editor: Anne Sahlin.
Printed by Robert Burton Printers (Sefton, NSW).

Distributed by Kirby Book Company Pty Ltd,
Private Bag 19, P.O. Alexandria 2015.

The author is grateful to all those manufacturers who provided information and photographs, and offers special thanks to Marc McInnes, Adrian Ryan and John Turner.

All rights reserved. No part of this publication may be reproduced, stored in retrieval form or transmitted in any form, or by any means without written permission from the publishers.

INTRODUCTION

Aussie cars — over 200 models from 131 manufacturers!
Nearly a century of car-building in Australia captured in words and photographs!
The large collection of cars in this book highlights the enormous amount of ingenuity and enterprise found downunder.
Every one of these car-building projects involved a large amount of thought, effort and expense. Some resulted in hundreds of thousands of sales, others sent their creators into bankruptcy.
Aussie Cars has a chronological format which enables the reader to follow the development of the car in Australia page by page. It contains the most detailed research into the subject yet conducted and a wide collection of photos, some published for the first time.
The author, Tony Davis, is a former Sydney newspaper reporter whose lifelong interest in cars led him into full-time motoring journalism.
He has written for a large number of newspapers and magazines, was General Editor of the acclaimed *Macquarie Dictionary of Motoring* and is currently working on several other motoring books.□

CONTENTS:

A SPECIAL NOTE ON POWER OUTPUT 8

WHAT IS AN AUSSIE CAR? 9

AUSSIE CARS (FROM 1880) 11

INDEX 189

ACKNOWLEDGMENTS 192

LEFT: 1970 Bolwell Nagari

A SPECIAL NOTE ON POWER OUTPUT

The power output figures given in this book are those announced by the manufacturer at the time each vehicle was released.

Unfortunately, different systems of measuring power have been used in Australia at various times. Each system will produce a different figure for the same engine. This means that an accurate power output comparison between cars of different eras is not possible.

In the early days of motoring, the most commonly used unit was the horsepower. The lack of an agreed method for measuring horsepower, however, led to the widespread use of an artificial system. This was instituted by the British Royal Automobile Club and was derived from a formula which included the bore diameter and the number of cylinders. It was expressed in rated horsepower (HP).

In the years before WW1, the rated horsepower provided a reasonable guide to an engine's power output, but as technology improved, so did efficiency. Engineers started to prefer brake horsepower (bhp), which is the power developed by an engine when spinning at a given speed, as measured by a dynamometer.

The US system of measuring brake horsepower, called SAE, became popular from the 1940s. An SAE figure (derived from test procedures developed by the Society of Automotive Engineers) provides the gross power output of an engine without the exhaust system and ancillary equipment fitted. The SAE system was preferred by some companies because it flattered the engine, allowing them to come up with favourable figures for publicity purposes.

During the early 1970s, there was a general industry trend in Australia towards net horsepower. Measured with most or all engine equipment attached, it provided a lower but more realistic indication of usable output. Nevertheless, there were still different test procedures for arriving at the net figure.

Since Australia changed to the SI Metric system in 1976, power has usually been given in net kilowatts, with 75 kW being approximately equal to 100 bhp. This is called 'installed power' and is based on an Australian standard similar to the German DIN system.

For this publication, we have converted all figures (except rated horsepower) to kilowatts and, as a general rule, you can assume that figures are 'gross' up to the mid-1970s, then 'net' until the 1980s when 'installed' figures became almost universal. Because rated HP figures are artificially derived, they cannot be converted to metric equivalents.□

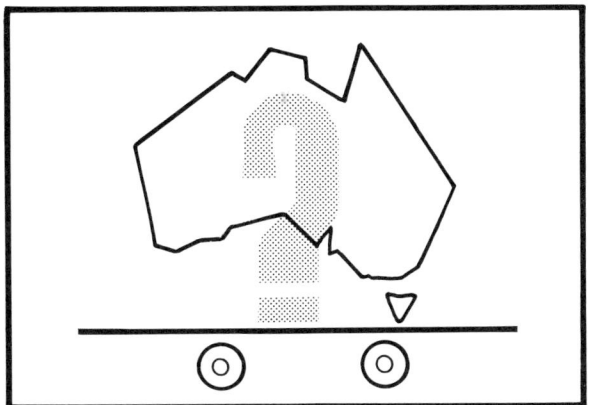

WHAT IS AN AUSSIE CAR?

Indeed! What the heck is an Aussie car? Where do you draw the line between cars built in Australia but designed overseas, cars partly made in Australia to local designs, and cars made overseas to Australian specifications?

Forced to draw the line somewhere, we chose to include:
* Production cars wholly or largely manufactured in Australia to local design.
* Production cars wholly or largely manufactured in Australia which are based on overseas models but have a reasonable amount of local design or engineering input.
* Production cars unique to Australia, irrespective of where the design or parts came from.
* Cars designed and built in Australia with the intention of producing them for on-road use.
* Cars designed and built in Australia of special historic or engineering interest.

Aussie Cars contains a run-down of every local model range released by the companies which were for so long Australia's 'Big Three' — Ford Australia, General Motors-Holden's and Chrysler Australia. Although Chrysler's early Valiants and Ford's early Falcons were almost identical to US models, they have been included because of their enormous impact on the local industry.

There have been some magnificent competition cars built in Australia, such as the Maybach and a string of Birranas, Elfins and Kaditchas. There have also been exquisite specials, 'one-off' custom machines and technically brilliant experimental cars like the Solar Trek and Flinders Electric car. Unfortunately, in this publication we cannot begin to fit all these in.

There's always another time. . . .

AUSSIE CARS
from 1880

1880 GILGEN

The Gilgen was a steam carriage said to have been built in South Australia around 1880.

If the story of the vehicle — which was first published in London in 1904 — is ever authenticated, the Gilgen will stand as Australia's first self-propelled road vehicle. Furthermore, it will show that motoring in Australia stretches back to the days before Daimler and Benz.

In 1904, 14 years after members of the British Royal Family had visited Australia, a member of the royal party, Mr C.A. Blake, related that they had visited a residence near Adelaide where a Swiss-born engineer named Gilgen showed them his homemade steamer. It had three wheels, could seat nine people and was powered by a 5 HP engine driving a three-speed gearbox. The top speed was given as 32 km/h.

According to Mr Blake, the local authorities had ordered the vehicle off the roads because it frightened horses.

Little is known about C.A. Blake. It seems that he was an Australian resident who owned a Thomson steam car shortly after the turn of the century and drove it a great distance.

His interest in cars adds some weight to his description of the Gilgen but unfortunately no photographs of the vehicle are known to exist.

Extensive research has so far failed to provide any further information.

1893 KNIGHT-EATON

Though essentially a powered bicycle, the 'Knight-Eaton' has the distinction of being the first petrol-engine-powered vehicle driven in Australia.

In 1893 Mr H. Knight-Eaton, who was manager of Brisbane's Austral Cycle Agency, built a small engine and mounted it behind the back of a pedal cycle.

The small machine was said to be unstable but, nevertheless, Mr Knight-Eaton used it for at least one journey.

In April 1896 Knight-Eaton demonstrated a benzol-engined two-wheeler in George Street, Sydney, and attracted a crowd of 5000 people.

1893 McINTOSH

The McIntosh is said to have taken to the roads around Picton, NSW, in 1893.

But, as in the case of the 1880 Gilgen, the only information is based on a published report made many years later. In 1946 a Mr McIntosh wrote a letter to the *Picton Post* claiming that in 1893 he had built a 'car'. He stated that he had mounted a steam engine and boiler on chassis rails and wheels and had driven the vehicle on public roads.

Though many references to the McIntosh have appeared over the years, no real evidence has been produced that the car was built as early as claimed.

1896 SHEARER

The Shearer was the first motorised four-wheeler publicly demonstrated in Australia.

More a 'carriage' than a 'car', the massive steam-powered vehicle was built over an 11-year period in Mannum, South Australia.

The builders were David and John Shearer, brothers engaged in the manufacture of agricultural machinery. They started work on their car in 1885, at a time when steam carriages were just beginning to appear in Europe and America, and Daimler and Benz had not announced their first petrol cars.

The Shearer, which could seat up to 12, was designed by David Shearer using many parts manufactured in the brothers' factory. These parts included a conventional steam engine (rated at 20 HP) and a rear axle which incorporated a full differential. The steering mechanism was remarkably modern, with a steering quadrant, draglinks, kingpins, stub axles and tie rods.

In 1896 the brothers made many journeys around Mannum (about 80 km from Adelaide), then took the carriage on a 160 kilometre journey without mishap.

In 1900 David Shearer was invited by the Adelaide Chamber of Manufacturers to exhibit the steamer. He needed special permission from the Mayor to bring his carriage into the city and was given strict instructions as to which roads he was permitted to use.

The Shearer carriage cruised at 24 km/h on level roads. Higher speeds were possible but the vehicle, with its ironclad wheels and primitive springing, became uncomfortable and difficult to handle.

The Shearer brothers made no more vehicles but concentrated on manufacturing farm equipment. They used their carriage for many years.

1897 PIONEER

The kerosene-fuelled Pioneer was once heralded by the press as 'Australia's First Horseless Carriage'.

It was launched with great zeal and photographs were published around the world.

The Pioneer had its beginnings when Henry Austin, an amateur inventor from Fitzroy, Victoria, designed a lightweight, petrol-fuelled engine. He wanted to follow it up by building a complete vehicle and 20 local businessmen formed the Australian Horseless Carriage Syndicate to back him.

Austin, however, withdrew from the project when the Syndicate pressured him to have the vehicle ready for exhibition at the February 1897 Melbourne Cycle Exhibition. The syndicate then hired Grayson Engineering to fit a single-cylinder, stationary-type engine under the driver's seat of what was little more than a horse-drawn carriage.

Magnificently painted and trimmed, the prototype Pioneer was capable of 16 km/h. A public demonstration was arranged in which Lord Brassey, Governor of Victoria, took several rides with ladies from Government House.

An article on the demonstration was published in the *Scientific Australian* of 20 March 1897, saying that Lord Brassey was 'well pleased' with the demonstration. This report included a mini 'road test' which stated: 'the driver ... has not only a brake and steering handle within easy access of his seat but also the stopping and starting handle. The petroleum engine gives no great evidence of either vibration or smell'.

Only one Pioneer was built. Several months after being exhibited it disappeared from sight, probably seized by a supplier in lieu of money owed by the Syndicate.

1897 HIGHLAND

The Sydney-made Highland was probably the first four-wheeler offered for sale in Australia.

Charles Highland was a Sydney cycle dealer who imported a Daimler petrol engine in 1894 and constructed a primitive motorised tricycle. Two years later Highland and his son, Charles Jnr, built a four-wheeled, two-seater vehicle using bicycle components and a De Dion-Bouton engine.

Replicas of this car were offered for sale in 1897 but it is not known how many were built. □

1897 PENDER-HERTEL

The Pender-Hertel was a US vehicle with an Australian-designed transmission.
Powered by a petrol engine, it was built for Victorian engineer John Pender and demonstrated locally in 1897.

Pender — primarily a manufacturer of horseshoe nails — visited Chicago in 1896 and was greatly impressed by a car designed and built by Max Hertel for the Chicago Times-Herald race.

Upon his return to Australia, Pender devised a new type of transmission (probably a friction drive unit) and sent the details to Hertel in the US. Hertel fitted a car with Pender's transmission and then shipped it to Australia where Pender offered replicas for sale. It is not known if any were completed.

Powered by a horizontally opposed two-cylinder engine located under the driver's seat, the Pender-Hertel had a maximum speed of 25 km/h.

1898 THOMSON

The Thomson, a small steam-powered vehicle built by Herbert Thomson of Armadale, Victoria, was the first Australian 'car' to make a interstate journey.

Herbert Thomson, a young electrical engineer, started work on his 5 HP steamer around 1896 and it was first driven two years later by Thomson and his cousin, Edward Holmes. The steamer made its public debut at the Malvern Cricket Ground in Melbourne in June 1898.

The Thomson was a four-seater with its body built from fiddleback ash and silky ash. Engineering features included side-lever steering and an extremely small steam engine of the vertical compound type. The Pioneer had chain-drive and its cart-like wheels were clad by Dunlop with the first pneumatic car tyres made in Australia.

In 1900, again accompanied by Holmes, Thomson took his car by boat to Sydney for display at the Royal Agricultural Show where it won a gold medal. Afterwards, they drove inland to Bathurst for the annual Agricultural Show. After this, the two men set out to drive to Melbourne.

The car completed the 790 km journey in ten days at an average running speed of 14 km/h, often travelling through floods, creeks and deep mud. Its speed ranged from 8 to 60 km/h, depending on the gradient of the road as well as its surface.

On completing his epic journey, Thomson formed the Thomson Motor Car Company Ltd and announced that he would put the car into production with a bigger engine, rated at 10 HP. He received 150 orders but only 12 cars were built. Two each were sold to the Melbourne Fire Brigade, Melbourne Post Office and the Tamworth Shire Council (NSW). The others were sold to private motorists.

1898 ZIEGLER

The Ziegler was an ambitiously conceived and meticulously built steam car constructed during the 1890s.

The designer and builder, Johann Ziegler of Allansford, Victoria, was a skilled machinist who learned his trade in his native Germany. He personally built almost every component in his steamer. Unlike most other designs of the era, Ziegler's had a small radiator to condense the steam back to water and so reduce the number of times the tank needed to be refilled.

Interestingly, this vehicle introduced what was probably the world's first automotive rear-view mirror. It was fitted not because there was a traffic problem in Allansford but because Ziegler needed to keep an eye on the boiler's water level gauge, mounted under the rear seat.

Ziegler built two identical machines. He kept one and used it for several years, the other was sold to defray the cost of materials for both cars.

After building these two cars, Ziegler established a company to produce and sell 'Zieglers'. Despite his intentions, it seems probable that no more cars were built.

1899 SUTTON

The small Melbourne-built Sutton was a pioneer front-wheel drive design.

It was powered by a single-cylinder engine driving the front wheels through a chain system. The steering, operated by a lever mounted on the side of the car, acted on all four wheels.

This unusual vehicle was designed by Henry Sutton, who in 1898 had built a two-cylinder three-wheeler for pacing racing cycles.

The 1899 Sutton four-wheeler captured space in the English press which published the mechanical specifications of this 'antipodean invention' and quoted Mr Sutton:

'It is a doctor's phaeton to seat two,' he said, 'but a box seat can be added over the motor to take a third person or luggage.'

The car was in many ways very advanced for its time and may have been the world's first car with front-wheel drive. Other features included an ignition system with an advance-and-retard mechanism and automatic engine oil lubrication. The Sutton also had a self-starter working on the recoil principle. It was intended to be produced in quantity by the Austral Otis Company but the cost proved too high.

Cars subsequently built by Sutton had conventional steering.

1900 FINLAYSON

The Finlayson brothers were responsible for the first motor vehicle built in Tasmania.

Working from a foundry in Devonport, they followed this by building another eight motor vehicles, including six buses, between 1900 and 1910.

The first Finlayson was a stylish steam-powered four-seater car with a two-cylinder 6 HP engine fuelled by kerosene. It had solid tyres and chain-drive. Apart from the wheels, the vehicle was entirely made in Devonport.

In 1904 the brothers built a larger car, fitting an imported two-cylinder 9 HP petrol engine to a chassis frame and body of their own manufacture. After selling this, the brothers built a four-seater car with a two-cylinder, horizontally opposed engine.

Their next machine was a bus which, except for the imported engine, was almost all their own work. After the bus had completed successful tests, the brothers built at least five more and sold them to Tasmanian transport firms.

1900 CAMPBELL

Tasmanian Archibald Campbell, a professional cycle maker and enthusiastic motorist, built three cars between 1900 and 1912.

Little is known about the cars other than the fact they included a four-seater steamer. In April 1904 Archibald Campbell made headlines when he raced the express train between Launceston and Hobart, driving one of his own cars. He won, covering the 170 km distance in 400 minutes, averaging 25.5 km/h.

1900 LEWIS

Vivian Lewis' Adelaide cycle firm made a series of small cars between 1900 and 1906, including what was claimed to be the first car built in South Australia.

After producing a motorised tandem cycle in 1898, Lewis teamed with Murray Aunger and Tom O'Grady in 1900 to build a single-cylinder, four-wheeled buggy. It had three seats, an aircooled engine and a two-speed transmission which drove the rear wheels via a chain. A tiller was used for steering.

This car was said to drive well on the level but often had to be pushed uphill.

Lewis followed this model with a series of light cars and a range of motorcycles. Although car production ceased in 1906, Lewis motorcycles continued to be made for several more years.

Murray Aunger was probably referring to a Lewis car, four decades later, when he wrote of a motoring experience he had shared with Lewis and O'Grady:

'An impression which remains in my memory was a run to Mount Barker ... to give an exhibition on the Mount Barker Showground. At the appointed time we puffed into the arena in great style amidst tumultuous cheering.

'After our hard run (and often walking) we thought that our efforts were to be rewarded by a little hero worship, but we were doomed to disappointment. We had only negotiated one round of the oval when the show suddenly developed into an uproar. Horses and cattle bolted at the terrific din made by our single-cylinder chain-driven vehicle and the objectionable smell we left in our trail.

'When things quietened down a little we were dismayed to find that the crowd were hooting us and demanding us to "get off", so we made a hurried exit for home.' □

1900 HAMMER

The Hammer was a lightweight car built about 1900 by cycle mechanic Bruno Hammer of Mount Torrens, South Australia.

Hammer had never seen a car when he was asked to build one for a client. He used imported drawings and built the entire vehicle himself, including the chassis, wheels, engine and carburettor. Few details have survived but probably only one Hammer was produced.□

1901 LEAN

Soon after the turn of the century, Richard Lean of Lithgow, NSW, started building a motor car.

Though a steam engineer by profession, he elected to use an imported De Dion petrol engine rated at 8 HP.

With assistance from locals he built a wooden chassis, then fitted four carriage wheels and a rather primitive steering system. Belt drive was used. No differential was fitted.

The vehicle is said to have cruised at 32 km/h on a trip from Lithgow to Bathurst. It seems from a report in *The Lithgow Mercury* newspaper that a local police sergeant managed to score himself a ride in the Lean under the pretext of checking that the vehicle was fitted with a safe stopping mechanism.

When cruising at 40 km/h, the sergeant commanded Lean to hit the brakes. The paper reported that following this command 'there was a jittering screech of iron on ground and then the strangled bellow of the sergeant as he sailed cleanly over the top of the motor and sprawled on his stomach in the dust'.

No more Leans are known to have been built.□

1901 TRACKSON

The Trackson was a Brisbane-built car which first ran in 1901.

The designer, James Trackson, was an intrepid motorist whose activities led him to be prosecuted several times for 'endangering the lives of citizens'.

Based on a De Dion car imported from France, the Trackson was powered by a 5 HP petrol engine and was said to be capable of 25 km/h. It was built at Trackson Bros Ltd, James Trackson's electrical firm, which produced a second car around 1904.

1901 TREVETHAN

Queensland's 1901 Trevethan was a kerosene-fuelled, chain-driven vehicle equipped with solid rubber tyres.

It was produced by a Toowoomba carriage-building company, under the supervision of the manager, Walter Trevethan.

The firm also produced a 6 HP buggy in 1904, using an imported engine.

1902 DAVIS

Mr R. 'Dick' Davis of Adelaide was one of several men experimenting with homemade cars at the turn of the century.

He differed from most as he completed his car, a four-seater with belt drive, and had it running by 1902. The Davis had a spring-mounted body and a 3 HP aircooled engine.

1902 BULLOCK

The Bullock was built in Adelaide by a professional cycle maker, John Bullock. It was a four-wheeler powered by a watercooled De Dion engine rated at 4 HP. John Bullock also made some motorcycles in the early years of the century and was said to have built a quadricycle powered by an aircooled 2½ HP engine in 1901.

1902 PHIZACKERLEY

The Phizackerley was built in Sydney by Mr I. Phizackerley.

Although later to become better known as a major seller of foreign cars, Phizackerly tried to launch a marque of his own shortly after the turn of the century.

He built several cars of his own design, including one which was exhibited at the 1902 Sydney Agricultural Show. Conventional in design, it was a two-seater powered by a single-cylinder 6 HP De Dion-Bouton engine coupled to a three-speed gearbox.

It was offered for sale but was too expensive to be competitive with imported models.

1903 PUCKRIDGE

The Puckridge was the work of F.B. Puckridge, a cycle maker living in the isolated fishing town of Port Lincoln, South Australia.

In 1903 Puckridge was asked by a neighbour, Dr Kinmont, to modify a powered tricycle. The doctor, who imported the vehicle from the Motor Manufacturing Company of England, had been hurt when the tricycle toppled over on a bend and he required a more stable vehicle.

Puckridge took the tricycle apart and built a four-wheeler, using the original single-cylinder 2.75 HP De Dion-type engine. He added a two-speed belt-drive transmission, tiller steering, gas lighting and fan cooling with a curious tunnel for induction. He also devised a starter system which involved pulling a chain through a hole in the floorboards to rotate the engine. The car had no differential.

Only one Puckridge was built.

1903 KNOWLES

The Knowles car was designed by A.J. Knowles, a Canadian who arrived in Sydney during the late 1890s.

Knowles came to Australia to start a branch of the Gold Bicycle Company. Around the turn of the century, he bought an 1899 De Dion-Bouton and fell under the spell of the automobile.

Soon after, Knowles decided to manufacture a car of his own design. He formed Knowles Automobile and Motor Power Company (in Bridge Sreet, Sydney) and in 1903 a prototype Knowles car was built, probably by Aster of Paris.

Knowles arranged for another French company, Darracq, to build the production car then leased a Melbourne showroom to assist in distribution. Very few Knowles cars were imported before Darracq officials persuaded A.J. Knowles to sell standard Darracq models in place of his own design.□

1903 INNES

Two different Innes cars were offered for sale in 1903 by a company controlled by George Innes, a pioneer Tasmanian motorist who had moved to Sydney.

Interestingly, Innes had been one of the first people in Australia to be booked for speeding. He was fined for travelling down a Sydney street at 13 km/h.

The Innes cars had locally made engines, one having a single cylinder, the other having four cylinders. Other parts were imported.

Two Innes cars were purchased by biscuit maker H.R. Arnott and used in the 1905 Dunlop Reliability Trial. Both completed the event. In 1919 a George Innes became a partner (with Charles Innes) in Sydney's Lincoln car-making venture. It was possibly the same man.□

1903 MODISTACH QUAD

The 'Quad' was built in Tanunda, South Australia, by a local blacksmith, Fred Modistach.

It was a four-wheeler with cycle forks holding its front wheels. Power came from a single-cylinder 4.5 HP imported Automotor.

The Quad was finished in 1903. No further cars were built by Modistach.

1903 RICHTER

The 1903 Richter car was remarkable for the fact that it had an infinitely variable drive system.

Although a few such cars had been built overseas, the Richter was almost certainly the first car with this feature built in Australia.

Chris Richter of Hawthorn, Victoria, built the small car using an imported two-cylinder aircooled petrol engine and a friction disc drive. By means of a control lever, the driver could move the friction disc across the face of another disc, gaining an infinite number of gear ratios in the forward or reverse direction.

Also unusual was a starting mechanism incorporating a system of ropes and pulleys that allowed the engine to be started from the driver's seat. The accelerator was operated by hand.

The car, said to be capable of 32 km/h, recorded a big mileage before Mr Richter sold it.

1903 MARRIOTT

The Marriott steam car was built around 1903 in Melbourne by James Marriott and his son Clarence.

Fitted with wooden artillery wheels, it used an English-made engine and ran on kerosene.

The design was an improvement on most steamers because it incorporated a water condenser to allow a greater cruising range on a tank of water. Few other details have survived.

Only one Marriott was built.

1903 TRESCOWTHICK 'QUAD'

Charles Trescowthick, a South Australian engineer, produced several small stationary engines at the turn of the century before building a car in 1903.

The first Trescowthick, a three-wheeler, was powered by a De Dion engine rated at 2½ HP and used other imported components. It carried a passenger sitting in a basket ahead of the driver.

Trescowthick, who was living in Angaston, in the Barossa Valley, then built two light four-wheelers, called 'Quads', probably in the same year.

Trescowthick went to Detroit in 1909 and was offered the importing rights to the new Model T Ford. He declined, reasoning that the car did not look rugged enough for Australian roads.

1904 OHLMEYER 'JIGGER'

The Ohlmeyer Jigger is a fine example of country ingenuity.

It was built by Albert Ohlmeyer, a watchmaker living in South Australia's Barossa Valley. Ohlmeyer was a keen motorcyclist and when, in 1904, he decided he wanted a car, he designed and built a simple four-wheeler, using whatever components he could buy or make.

The Olymeyer had cycle wheels and a chassis frame made from hickory bearers. It was fitted with a single-cylinder, British-built Automotor engine which had been used to drive a stationary water pump. This engine was mounted at the front of the vehicle and drove the rear wheels by means of a flat belt which turned a pair of pulleys on a rear countershaft. Chains and sprockets on each end of the countershaft transferred the drive to the back wheels.

The drive system supplied power to only one wheel at a time, the nearside wheel being driven by a low ratio sprocket, the offside wheel by a high ratio sprocket. This arrangement eliminated the need for a differential. The countershaft also carried a pulley — for use as a footbrake — and a clutch to engage top gear.

Ohlmeyer made do without a suspension system, hence the name 'Jigger'. The only 'springing' was provided by the soft tyres and the whip of the hickory bearers.

The Jigger could seat two. It had an overall length of 2.8 metres, weighed 230 kg, could cruise at 32 km/h and, under favourable conditions, clock 40 km/h. Albert Ohlmeyer used the car regularly from 1904 until 1923 and his sons — Jule and Ernst — used it intermittently until 1969. By that time it had covered over 65 000 km with only one major breakdown.

1904 HUMBLE

The Humble was built by Humble & Sons, a Geelong-based foundry firm which had provided engineering assistance to the builders of the Pioneer (in 1897) and which built buses and trucks from 1903.

The rear-entrance Humble car was exhibited at the 1904 Melbourne Royal Show. A four-seater with a single-cylinder De Dion engine, it was too expensive to be successful and never went into serious production.

Humble & Sons was purchased by Buckingham & Ward in 1933 to manufacture the four-cylinder engine for the Buckingham car. □

1904 FLOOD SEDAN

William James Flood was an English-born automobile body-builder who built Australia's first fully enclosed sedan.

Shortly after arriving in Melbourne, Flood went to work for Harley Tarrant's body works. In 1904 an unusual car was commissioned by Dr W.K. Bouton who wanted full weather protection while doing his rounds. James Flood was given the job of designing and building the body. The result was a finely crafted sedan built on a Fiat chassis.

Dr Bouton was so pleased with the body that in later years he had it transferred to a more modern chassis.

In 1907 James Flood founded what became one of Australia's largest body-building firms. This company was still in business during the 1980s. □

1904 MAYMAN

The Mayman car was the work of Charles Mayman, a young and very skilled Melbourne engineer.

Charles Mayman built several motorcycles before making his first car. These motorcycles included one which was ridden to an Australian speed record in 1904 by Dunlop's publicity manager Harry James. In that same year Mayman, who was only 20 years old, used drawings published in a British journal as the basis for his first car.

The Mayman four-wheeler was made to an exceptionally high standard and successfully competed in a run organised by the Automobile Club of Victoria. It was powered by a single-cylinder 6 HP De Dion engine and had two forward speeds.

Mayman was killed in a motorcycle accident late in 1904 and no further Mayman cars were made. The original model had been built while Mayman was working for E. Beauchamp (who ran a successful cycle firm) and was sometimes called the 'Beauchamp'.

1904 ACE

The firm of Holding & Overall in Sydney built a 10 HP two-seater motor buggy called Ace in 1904.

Little is known about the Ace, but in 1916 the same company built a car called Acme.

1904 AUSTRALIA

Despite the grandiose name, the Australia was a fairly unexciting vehicle. Designed and built in 1904 by Sydney engineer Albert Woods, it was a single-seater with a two-cylinder engine. No further models were produced.

1904 NIELSEN

In 1905 the Nielsen company of Rockhampton, Queensland, advertised that it could supply 'motor cars built to order, suitable for this district'.

This followed the building of a prototype car in 1904 by Danish-born coachbuilder A. Nielsen. Nielsen had moved to Queensland in 1873 to start his own business as a 'separation coach, waggon and motor works'. He exhibited two horse-drawn carriages and a four-wheeled motorised vehicle at the Rockhampton Show in 1904.

It is not known how many Nielsen cars were built.

1905 EARNSHAW

The Earnshaw car was produced entirely within the small town of Echuca, Victoria, in 1905.

The designer and builder was Captain Charles Earnshaw, a local inspector of paddle-steamers, who probably used US plans. For the mechanical components, Earnshaw made his own casting patterns, using local facilities and the foundry which serviced the paddle-steamers.

Timber was used for the main chassis frame members. The two-cylinder, four-seater car was used in the Echuca area for many years.

1905 CLEMENTS

The Clements was built by Sydney motorist H.I. Clements in 1905. The design was heavily flawed and production never proceeded.

1905 McDONALD

In 1905 Alfred McDonald, a builder of farming equipment (including stationary engines) operating in Glenferrie, Victoria, built a primitive petrol-powered vehicle.

It had a 6 HP vertical engine, friction disc transmission and chain-drive. No body was fitted.

1905 TARRANT

The superbly crafted Tarrant car was the basis of the most ambitious early attempt to launch an Australian motor industry. It was also the first Australian car to win a motor race.

The Tarrant was the brainchild of Victorian-born Harley Tarrant, who had built an internal-combustion engine in the 1890s.

Tarrant's first attempt at car making was in 1897 when he built a motorised buggy. It was not a success but a year later he launched the Harley Tarrant Motor Syndicate. The new company's main line was manufacturing stationary engines but, in 1901, in partnership with Howard Lewis, Tarrant designed and built a lightweight car with a 6 HP Benz engine.

A third man, Bill Ross, joined the partners and they started selling imported cars. Recognising the need for local production, Tarrant set up Melbourne Motor Body Works, later to become Victoria's largest body-building operation.

Still determined to launch his own car, Tarrant built a two-cylinder 8 HP model in 1903. This car won Australia's first recognised car race, held at Sandown Park in March 1904. Tarrant also won the 1905 Dunlop Reliability Trial driving an Argyll. He entered his own 8 HP car in the second Dunlop Trial (also held in 1905) and was among five men declared joint winners. His next venture was a four-cylinder 14/16 HP tourer, which he intended to produce in volume.

Tarrant showed it was possible to produce a car in Australia which was every bit as good as imported models. But despite his eagerness, engineering ability and business acumen, he found it impossible to compete on price. Only 16 Tarrants were built over a ten-year period.

Tarrant later made a fortune selling Model T Fords. He lived until 1949, his ninetieth year.

1905 TOY

The Toy was designed and built by William Toy, an engineer living at Dandenong, Victoria.

Powered by a two-cylinder engine rated at 8 HP, it had a two-speed gearbox and chain-drive to the rear wheels. The light two-seater car was notable as all components, except the carburettor, wheel rims and tyres, were made by Mr Toy.

Mr Toy completed the car in 1905 and used it for his personal transport.

1906 TAYLOR

The three-wheeled Taylor was built in Wollongong by Mr F.A. Taylor.

Mr Taylor, a cycle maker by trade, imported many components from England but designed and built the body himself. The vehicle, which was completed in 1906, was driven by belts and chains and was said to be capable of 40 km/h.

1906 JESSOP

The Jessop steam car was produced around 1906 in the township of Scottsdale, Tasmania.

Though the four-seater carriage-like vehicle was impressive, production never got under way.

1906 TILL

The small Till car was an early 'one-off' two-seater built by William Till, a Melbourne engineer.

It was completed in 1906. Almost all the components were imported.

1906 AUSTRALIS

A range of vehicles carrying the Australis name was built and sold from around the turn of the century until 1907.

They were the product of the Australia Motor Company, a subsidiary of G.W. & G. Wood, based at the Sydney suburb of Leichhardt.

In 1897 G.W. & G. Wood had built a four-wheeled cyclecar powered by a De Dion engine. The company followed this with a locally-made engine in 1897 and shortly afterwards, the Australia Motor Company was formed with a view to volume production. In 1901 the new company offered a small two-seater with a single-cylinder 3 HP watercooled engine.

By 1906 the Australia Motor Company was producing a limited number of four-seater vehicles with two-cylinder 7 HP engines. Production ceased in 1907.

1906 SYME

The Syme was an early Melbourne-built vehicle intended for volume production.

Advertisements for the Syme were first published in 1906. Made by Syme Engineering & Motor Pty Ltd, it was a chain-driven, single-cylinder, four-wheeled vehicle. Probably only three or four were built.

1906 GRAYSON

The Grayson car was built by the Melbourne-based Grayson engineering company, which had been involved in the construction of the Pioneer car in 1897.

The 1906 Grayson car used a four-cylinder 19.6 HP engine. Little is known about the design but the Grayson received considerable publicity when it was used to take the Governor of Victoria to the Melbourne Cup.

1906 DAY

Built in Melbourne in 1906, the Day was not so much a car as a powered billycart.

Racing driver Jack Day constructed the vehicle so that he could compete in motor races conducted on a banked cycle track. Although primitive in design, it was possibly Australia's first purpose-built racing car.

1906 ANDERSON

The Anderson was a 'one-off' produced in Richmond, Victoria, around 1906 by the company of W. Anderson & Sons.

1907 SWINNERTON

The 1907 Swinnerton was possibly the world's first car without a separate chassis.

The small vehicle was designed and built at Rozelle (Sydney) by Alfred Swinnerton, who personally made every component, including the castings for the four-cylinder 11 HP engine. Drive was provided to the rear wheels by belts and the body was made from American hickory wood.

Mr Swinnerton also single-handedly built a bigger car in 1915 (see separate entry). □

1907 NORMAN

Mr W. A. Norman, an Adelaide machinist, is said to have built a car around 1907.

It was a three-wheeled, four-cylinder affair using a mixture of self-made and imported components. □

1908 HAINES & GRUT

Haines & Grut, a very early Melbourne vehicle builder, produced at least five motorised buggies.

During the 1890s C.W. Kellow and Howard Lewis were in partnership in a small firm which serviced and imported cars and built a few motorcycles. When Lewis left in 1897 to join Harley Tarrant, Tommy Haines joined the firm. After gaining some experience, he teamed with P. J. Grut, a local estate agent to make a buggy for local production.

The new business operated out of a'Beckett St, Melbourne. Its first vehicle, a buggy built in 1908, had tiller steering but at least four more were made with conventional steering wheels. All were wholly Australian, apart from the hickory wheels which came from the US and the French-built Longuemare carburettor. The engine, made by a Melbourne engineering company, was a horizontally opposed, two-cylinder 10 HP watercooled unit.

An unusual drive system used chains between the engine and a countershaft which drove both rear wheels by means of canvas-covered steel cables. Slight slippage of the cables eliminated the need for a differential.

The Haines & Grut used wood, strengthened by steel, for both its body and chassis.

An advertisement claimed: 'This buggy will commend itself to Doctors, Commercial Travellers, Business Men and others ... It is light, serviceable, strong ... easily driven and inexpensive in its up-keep'. □

1908 CRAINE

The Craine was built in 1908 by a Melbourne body builder T.C. Craine.
He designed a motorised buggy using an imported two-cylinder 12 HP, horizontally opposed engine and a three-speed gearbox. 'Craines' were offered with a choice of body styles and several were sold.

1908 ROSSITER

Herbert Rossiter, a young engineering apprentice from Carlton in Victoria, is said to have built a small steam-powered vehicle around 1908.
No details have survived.

1909 COTTON

Unrelated to the car built in 1914 by Sidney Cotton, the 1909 Cotton was designed and commissioned by Queenslander Alfred John Cotton.
The prototype was built in England and shipped to Queensland in 1910. The design was fairly primitive but had several features, including a power take-off, intended to make it suitable for use by farmers. Plans were made to sell Cotton cars in Australia but it is not known how many, if any, were sold.

1910 HUSBAND

The unusual Husband car was made in Charters Towers, Queensland, around 1910 by motor engineer Norman Husband.
It incorporated an unusual friction transmission, designed by Mr Husband, which allowed the engine to run at a constant speed regardless of road speed. Another unusual design feature was the use of three torsion bars on each side of the chassis frame to reduce twisting on rough roads.
The Husband had simple but effective rack-and-pinion steering. The American-made Holsman engine which powered the car was a horizontally opposed, two-cylinder unit. The friction transmission provided the variation in road speed and heavy chains drove the rear wheels.
The car originally had buggy wheels and a buggy body.
According to later reports, the friction transmission was not a great success and Husband did not build any further cars.

1911 HOLDEN

Roy H. Holden was a young engineering student in Geelong, Victoria, when he built a small, single-seater steam car in 1911.

Mr Holden had nothing to do with the famous car later produced by GM-H, but preceded both General Motors Australia and Holden's Motor Body Builders.

With the aid of some friends, he constructed a lightweight steam car which had a steel frame, pram wheels and a simple drive system turning one rear wheel only. The boiler had a very small capacity and, although the car actually ran, it had little more than novelty value.

Roy Holden later established a successful car sales and engineering business. In 1948 when GM-H launched what they said was the first Holden, Roy Holden wrote to GM in the US to set the record straight. They sent back a gilt-edged scroll acknowledging his achievement.

1912 AUSTRALIAN FOUR

The Australian Four was a local variation on the British Wolseley 1.1-litre car. It was built around 1912 by F.H. Gordon & Company of Sydney.

The company's director, Frederick Hugh Gordon, later launched the ambitious Australian Six project.

1913 B & B

The B & B cyclecar was made by the Sydney engineering firm, Bennett and Barkell.

It had an aircooled two-cylinder engine, a three-speed gearbox and worm-drive. Probably only one was built.

1913 CALDWELL-VALE

The innovative Caldwell-Vale was the world's first touring car with four-wheel drive (4WD).

The man responsible was Felix Caldwell, one of Australia's great early automotive engineers. Felix had designed and built a range of engines for cars and trucks from 1909, and in 1910 had fitted four-wheel brakes to a vehicle (possibly a world first) and invented the tipper truck.

Some of the trucks he designed and built before WW1 had 4WD and four-wheel power-assisted steering.

Working with his brother Norman, Felix first devised and patented a 4WD/4WS system in 1907. After four years the brothers had refined the design and found a financial backer in Henry Vale, a Sydney locomotive maker.

At first the system was applied to a series of trucks and over the next few years 50 complete vehicles were manufactured.

The prototype passenger tourer had a 30 HP engine, 4WD and 4WS. The model was tested on the Botany Bay sandhills in August 1913 and observers said the car was so impressive it could climb steep, sandy hills and take sharp corners at 60 km/h.

Sadly, the Caldwell-Vale tourer never went into production. Its announcement co-incided with a lawsuit launched by a Queensland mining company. The company claimed to have lost large amounts of money when two 4WD trucks broke down in Burketown, on the Gulf of Carpentaria. The ensuing court battle — settled in the plaintiff's favour — effectively sent Caldwell-Vale bankrupt.

A company called Purcell Engineering took over Caldwell-Vale's assets and kept making 4WD trucks until the early 1920s. Purcell did not, however, build any further examples of the remarkable Caldwell-Vale car.

1913 MACQUE

The Macque passenger car, built in 1913, was intended for volume production.

A lightweight two-seater based on a quadricycle design, it was built by the Melbourne engineering firm of Allan Macqueen. It was offered with an aircooled or watercooled engine coupled to a friction-type transmission with belt drive to the rear wheels. Though grandiose hopes were held for the Macque, few were sold.

1913 AUSTRAL

Built in Geelong, Victoria, around 1913, the Austral was a cyclecar powered by a two-cylinder petrol engine.

Fitted with a friction drive transmission, it used side-mounted pulley belts to provide the final drive.

It is believed that three Australs were built.

1914 COTTON

The 1914 Cotton was the work of 20-year-old Sidney Cotton, who was later to become famous as an inventor.

It was built at a time when Cotton was working at the Dalkeith sheep station, Cassilis, NSW. The station owner sent Cotton to Sydney to buy parts to make a car for the station and after nine months work, the young employee drove the chassis to Brisbane. In Brisbane the Willys Overland agents built a body for it.

Cotton later designed the Sidcot flying suit (which was used by the RAF and RAAF) and became a pioneer in aerial and colour photography.

1914 TURNBULL

Steam engineers Arthur and Henry Turnbull are said to have built a car in 1914 in Surrey Hills, Victoria.

No information on the vehicle has survived but it is known that a 'Turnbull' steam-powered truck was later built, probably about 1918.

1915 SWINNERTON

The 1915 Swinnerton was designed and built at Rozelle (Sydney) by Alfred Swinnerton, who had built his first car in 1907 (see separate entry).

As with his first effort, the 1915 car was built without a separate chassis and Mr Swinnerton personally made every component, including the castings for the engine. The engine was described as 'the first semi-diesel, Hot Type engine to be made in Australia'. Presumably this meant it was a high-compression unit.

The 1915 Swinnerton was a two-seater tourer with an 11 HP engine and belt drive to the rear wheels. The prototype was driven for 72 000 kilometres during 10 years of use, but no more examples were built.

Among his many other achievements, Mr Swinnerton designed and built loudspeakers and patented a new type of 'blower' for pipe organs. He is said to have performed some engineering work on the 1919 Australian Six.□

1916 ACME

The Acme was a 10 HP car built by the Sydney firm of Holding & Overall, which had built a motor buggy called Ace in 1904.

Holding & Overall purchased the Acme Motor Engineering Works from G.S. Pursey and launched the Acme in 1916. It was not a success and few were made.

1916 EKINS

The Ekins was built single-handedly by South Australian gunsmith Archibald L. Ekins.

He became a motoring enthusiast after purchasing a second-hand New Orleans car in 1910 and, in 1916, built a vehicle of his own design. This was powered by an 8 HP two-stroke engine and used a friction drive system patented by Ekins.

No further models were produced.

1916 TUTTLE

The steam-powered Tuttle car was built by William Tuttle in Shepparton, Victoria, in 1916.

Fitted with a kerosene-burning engine mounted under the driver's seat, it had a metal body of carriage-like appearance.

In about 1918, Mr Tuttle is believed to have built a two-cylinder petrol-engined cyclecar.

1917 ROO

The Roo was the basis of an ambitious attempt to launch an Australian-made car during WW1.

It was backed by racing driver Rupert Jeffkins, who had been the riding mechanic for the legendary Ralph de Palma in the 1912 Indianapolis 500 and who claimed to have driven for Benz and Mercedes factory racing teams in Europe.

In keeping wth the patriotic feelings of the times, Roo Motor Manufacturing Company of Pitt Street, Sydney, went to great lengths to emphasise that its car was locally designed and built. The engine — rated at 10 HP — was a two-cylinder unit built by a Sydney engineer, Bill Foulis.

A prototype, with a sports body, was driven to Melbourne by Jeffkins and Foulis with the words 'The Roo, The Pioneer Car of Australia' written on the side. The pair attracted a lot of attention; by the time they arrived in Melbourne, the bodywork was graced with the autographs of 300 people who had inspected the car during the trip.

The Roo Manufacturing Company purchased a large site to build a factory in the suburb of Burwood and planned mass production. The brand was launched by Sydney Lord Mayor Meagher in September 1917.

Jeffkins' plan to manufacture every component for the Roo lead to delays and other problems. Only two cars were completed during the first year. A third was underway when a solicitor financing the Roo pulled out, causing the collapse of the venture.

1917 PALM

Although advertised as being 'ideally designed for Australian roads' and 'the car that all Australia is talking about', the Palm was really a modified Ford Model T.

Fitted with locally made mudguards, hubcaps and a distinctive radiator, it was produced and marketed by E.W. Brown Motors Ltd of Melbourne.

This company had had a long association with motorcycles and had launched its own brand, the EWB, early in 1912.

The mechanical components of the Palm were imported from Ford in the US, probably as spare parts, and were modified for right-hand drive. Sales were slow, especially since the Palm sold for almost twice the price of a standard Model T.

Ford launched a court action alleging patent infringement and the sale of Ford products without due acknowledgment; Palm production ceased shortly afterwards. It is not known how many were built.

A particularly handsome variation of the Palm was launched as the 'Renown' in the early 1920s. It had a unique body, Rolls-Royce-style radiator shell and nickel fittings throughout.

Without acknowledging the Ford antecedents, Renown cars were advertised as 'manufactured in the largest workshop in the world ... by the Master Hand'. For reasons mainly related to price, Renowns sold poorly.

During the mid-1920s, Brown was linked with yet another variation of the Model T. Called Spark, it was built by a Sydney company, using the radiator and many other features designed for the Renown. Production ran to about ten units.

1919 AUSTRALIAN SIX

Despite good looks and excellent engineering, the Australian Six was one of the great failures of motoring history.

The story started when Frederick Hugh Gordon, a motor trade figure who claimed to have imported and sold the first Ford in Australia, reasoned that a locally assembled car could sell for much less than comparable imported models. In 1917 Gordon visited the US and met Louis Chevrolet who, 'at great expense', gave not only engineering advice but the names of all companies supplying parts for the Chevrolet Light Six.

In 1918 Gordon returned to the US and placed orders for components to build the first 150 Australian Six chassis at his Sydney plant. His plan was to progressively introduce locally manufactured parts.

After considerable teething problems, Gordon produced 49 vehicles in 1919. They were fitted with local steel and timber bodies, US-built 3.7-litre, six-cylinder 34 kW Rutenber engines and Grant Lees gearboxes.

The Australian Six had a 3.1 metre wheelbase and a maximum speed of 100 km/h. It returned a fuel consumption figure of about 23 litres per 100 kilometres. The distinctive radiator was guaranteed not to boil.

Production increased during the next three years but, while Gordon's price was rising progressively, the Model T Ford was undercutting every car on the market.

Fighting bankruptcy, Gordon introduced improvements in 1923 and 1924, but the end was in sight. The firm of Harkness and Hillier tried to recoup debts by taking over the operation and moving to a smaller factory. A more powerful OHV Ansted engine was introduced and the 'Six' was driven to a new Sydney-Darwin speed record by Don Harkness.

The world depression signalled the end. The last few Australian Sixes were sold in 1930. About 900 had been made and the firm had lost 1000 pounds ($2000) on each one.□

1919 LINCOLN

The Lincoln was conceived and marketed by Charles Innes, who believed he could create a vast Australian motor industry. He set up distributors in Java, Japan, New Zealand and all Australian States before launching his car in 1919.

Unrelated to the Lincoln produced in the US, the Australian car was powered by an imported Continental six-cylinder engine, driving the rear wheels through a Detroit brand three-speed gearbox.

Innes chose the name for his car during a 1918 visit to America. After making arrangements with component suppliers, he built a prototype in Detroit and, in a much publicised 'test', drove it along the then unfinished Lincoln Highway to the Pacific coast, via the Great Salt Lake Desert.

Back home, Innes quickly ran into trouble — his uninsured factory burned down under suspicious circumstances. He borrowed more money, rented another factory and persevered. But his production was so small, the Lincoln sold at twice the price of a Model T Ford.

Although the Lincoln used mainly American-made components at first, the local content soon rose, with a Sydney firm supplying many parts. The design was entirely conventional, apart from buffalo hide seats and an unusual suspension system offered as an option. Called Cantilever Springing, it consisted of three long semielliptic springs running from the front to back on each side of the chassis.

In October 1921 a Lincoln Six was driven from Brisbane to Sydney and back with no more trouble than a change of tyres. It averaged a fuel consumption figure of 14.1 litres per 100 km.

The story of the Lincoln is very similar to that of the Australian Six. Both cars saw their prices rise and sales fall as the 1920s progressed. To add to Innes' problems, Ford acquired the US-based Lincoln company in 1922, and launched a lawsuit to prevent him using the same name. Innes eventually won the case but agreed to change his car's name to Lincoln Pioneer Six.

The Lincoln plant closed in 1926, after about 200 cars had been built.

1920 CARTER

The South Australian-built Carter was launched in prototype form in 1920.
Two four-cylinder models were displayed at the Adelaide Motor Show, being virtually short and long wheelbase variations on the same theme. Both were powered by imported engines and gearboxes but it was planned to make the body and the rest of the components in Australia.
Production did not proceed.

1920 VICHIE

The first Vichie was built in 1920 by Jim Vichie of Bundaberg, Queensland.
Vichie, an agricultural machinery engineer, followed his first car with a series of small vehicles incorporating self-constructed components as well as parts from a wide variety of English and American cars.
In his final car — a small coupe built just after WW2 — Vichie fitted a horizontally opposed two-cylinder engine of his own design and manufacture.

1921 WEGE

The Wege car was built around a very promising 'valveless' engine designed in Adelaide.

In 1920 William Wege and Charles Deland of Peterborough, South Australia, designed and patented a three-cylinder, two-stroke engine. This engine, which used an unusual but efficient scavenging system, was followed by a V-6 version and several of these were built for the partnership by Valveless Motors of Sydney.

The V-6 was extensively tested in a car designed and built by William Wege in 1921. It proved extremely good, being light, flexible and powerful. It was claimed that 'the oil consumption worked out at between 2000 and 3000 miles to the gallon'.

Wege sold the rights to the car to a firm known as the Adelaide Syndicate, which sent him to England to gain further experience in manufacturing techniques.

Some Wege engines were made for stationary and marine work and, upon William Wege's return from England in 1928, the Adelaide Syndicate announced plans to mass produce cars in South Australia. The onset of the Depression, however, finished the project and it is probable that no cars (other than the original prototype) were completed.

Later an in-line, six-cylinder version of the two-stroke engine was approved for aircraft use but production plans were dropped.

Meanwhile the original Wege car was driven more than 400 000 kilometres during the 1920s and 1930s. □

1922 SUMMIT

Advertised as a 'New Wonder Car' and 'An Australian Triumph', the Summit was built in Alexandria (Sydney) by Kelly's Motors Ltd between 1922 and 1926.

It was equipped with a radio, cigar lighter and electric stop lights. The car also came with 12 months warranty, another unusual feature in 1922.

The Summit was a conventionally engineered five-seater tourer, powered by a 3.4-litre, four-cylinder Lycoming side-valve engine.

Although most mechanical components were imported from the US, one option was an unusual locally designed suspension system.

This used a series of leaf springs running the full length of each side of the chassis frame and was said to provide an exceptionally smooth ride. Although described as 'unique Acme Patent Spring Suspension', this system was almost certainly similar to that offered on the Australian Lincoln (built from 1919). Unfortunately the long springs were prone to failure.

Only a few Summits were built.

1922 ALBANI SIX

The Albani Six was an impressive six-cylinder tourer built in Melbourne by Albani Motor Constructions Pty Ltd around 1922.

The prototype, fitted with a US-built 25 HP Continental engine, underwent an endurance test in which it covered 8000 kilometres in 12 days with its bonnet sealed. Engineers reported it suffered no serious mechanical or structural faults.

The car later completed the 1600 km Alpine Trial but, despite its many attributes, the Albani Six never went into volume production.

1922 ECO

The Eco was a Melbourne-assembled car planned for mass production and export.

It was designed by G. Hamilton-Grapes, using an imported 2.9-litre, four-cylinder Lycoming engine. The prototype was built in Detroit in 1921 and Ecos were assembled in Oakleigh, Victoria, during 1922 and 1923. Only a few were built before the project collapsed.

The Eco name was short for 'Economiser'. Hamilton-Grapes had designed a special manifold and carburettor which he claimed would ensure 35 miles per gallon (8 litres per 100 km).

The Eco had several unusual features for its time. These included adjustable front seats and the use of an aluminium alloy for the wheels and some other components. The spare wheel was housed inside the car.

1922 SOUTHERN SIX

Soon after WW1, Australian-British Motors Ltd was formed to make the Southern Six car.

The man behind it was flying ace Cyril Maddocks, a friend and former partner of Charles Kingsford Smith.

The Southern Six was powered by a 20 HP British-made Sage 2.4-litre, six-cylinder engine and incorporated other British components including Sankey wheels and a Wrigley gearbox. The body was built locally.

There was also talk of building a four-cylinder 'Southern Four' version. The prototype — a Six — was extensively tested and was was said to have a top speed of nearly 100 km/h and to use only 4.5 litres of petrol per 100 kilometres.

No other Southern cars are known to have been completed.☐

1923 CHIC

Advertised as a 'Car for Australian Conditions', the Chic was made at King's Park, Adelaide, between 1923 and 1929.

In spite of the nationalistic sales pitch, the car used a British chassis with an Australian body. It was designed by Clarence Chick and sold with a choice of two Meadows overhead valve engines: a 2.1-litre, four-cylinder unit developing 30 kW and a 2.7-litre, six-cylinder design of 36 kW.

At least 50 Chics were sold.☐

1923 MARKS-MOIR

The Marks-Moir was a highly original design which became the basis of the Southern Cross, built in 1933 by a syndicate headed by famous aviator Sir Charles Kingsford Smith.

The Marks-Moir was conceived by a Sydney dentist, Dr A.R. Marks, who in 1923 had the car built to his specifications in Britain and shipped to Sydney, where it served as his personal transport.

Two or three more Marks-Moir cars were built in Strathfield, NSW, including a second one for Dr Marks.

The design employed a unique chassis-less construction in which stressed plywood was used to provide a unitary structure. This was said to be exceptionally strong and therefore ideal for 'colonial conditions'.

The Marks-Moir's four-cylinder engine sat east-west across the chassis, close to the centre for optimum weight distribution. The car featured a two-speed epicycle transmission (probably from a Model T Ford) coupled to a conventional two-speed driving ratio, giving four forward speeds without the need for a clutch pedal. Chains drove the back axle through an unusual type of limited-slip differential.

Dr Marks was a principal of Motories, a Sydney motor house, and had been an avid motorist since 1903. One of his Mark-Moir cars passed on to his son, Jim Marks, who later went into partnership with Kingsford Smith to build an updated version based on the same unitary construction principle (see 1933 Southern Cross).☐

1923 SULMAN-SIMPLEX

The low-slung Sulman-Simplex was a small-engined cyclecar built by a Sydney company partly owned by racing driver Tom Sulman.

Sulman built the extremely lightweight vehicle and fitted it with a discarded motorcycle engine. This prototype made its debut at the Victoria Park racetrack in Sydney, when Tom Sulman drove it to second place in a feature race.

Full-scale production of the Sulman-Simplex was planned, using US-built two-cylinder aircooled engines. This did not eventuate.□

1925 BESST SUPER FOUR

The Besst Super Four was built in South Australia during the mid-1920s using local and imported components.

It was conceived by G.M. May of May's Motor Works in Adelaide.

May imported US-built 3.2-litre, four-cylinder Lycoming engines (rated at 19.6 HP), Muncie gearboxes and other parts, and made his own chassis frames. The bodies — described as 'King of the Road' five-seaters — were built in the Adelaide factory of T.J. Richards (which was later incorporated into Chrysler Australia).

The conventionally engineered Besst Super Four featured in advertisements promised 'a new appreciation of motoring ease and security'. Unfortunately, the Besst cost twice as much as an imported car of equivalent size and performance. About five were built and sold.□

1926 'GEELONG' MODEL T FORD

Once introduced to Australia, the low-priced, tough and durable Model T Ford took only a few years to become an institution. And an Australian.

By the 1920s Model Ts were built in Australia using locally designed and built bodies and many locally fabricated mechanical parts.

Henry Ford had introduced the Model T in the US in 1908 and hit a perfect formula for the day. Using a simple design and new assembly-line techniques, he was able to undersell his competitors and produce his cars at an unprecedented rate.

The Model T was powered by a conventional 22.5 HP, 2.9-litre, four-cylinder engine, giving a top speed of 72 km/h and fuel economy of 9.4 litres per 100 kilometres.

The Model T had a wheelbase of 2800 mm and was sold in Australia with a choice of five body styles, ranging from a two-seater runabout to a six-seater town car. The standard tourer was so bare of equipment that it weighed only 760 kg.

The Model T proved remarkably rugged and became so popular with Aussie farmers that it was dubbed the 'Squatter's Joy'.

Model T Fords were assembled in each State by different distributors until 1925 when the Ford Motor Company of Australia was established. With its base in a disused wool store in Geelong, Victoria, the new company built 12 500 Model Ts during its first full year. Most components came from Canada and advertisements of the day stated the Model T was 'fully made in the British Empire'. By late 1925 all local Model Ts were assembled by Ford Australia and these became known as 'Geelong' models.

In 1928 the Model T was finally replaced by the more sophisticated Model A. By that time, roughly 250 000 Model Ts had been sold in Australia and 90 000 in New Zealand. □

1929 GMA CHEVROLET (HOLDEN BODY)

During the 1920s and early 1930s, Chevrolets assembled by General Motors Australia Pty Ltd were fitted with locally designed bodies made by Holden's Motor Body Builders.

Holden's had been producing car bodies since 1917 and, by introducing modern equipment and new designs which required a minimum of hand finishing, it was able to undercut its rivals. By the 1920s the company had contracts for bodies not only for the locally assembled Chevrolet and other GMA cars, but for Dodge, Fiat, Chrysler, Studebaker, Overland, Hupmobile, Essex, Dort and Durant cars.

The name Holden was first used when English migrant James Alexander Holden set up a leather and saddlery business in Adelaide in 1854. This firm became Holden & Frost, which expanded to the point where it was building horse-drawn carriages and coaches. When Henry Frost died, James Holden's son Henry bought out his interest. In 1917 Holden was one of several companies which seized the golden opportunity to become body builders when the Australian government placed a severe limit on the import of complete motor vehicles.

By 1924 Holden accounted for half of Australia's total production of motor bodies, with an output of 22 150. The company invested in the most modern plant of its type in the southern hemisphere and produced 36 171 bodies in 1926. The world depression caused a huge drop in demand and, in 1931, Holden's output fell to a mere 1651 units, causing large losses.

General Motors Australia also ran into financial difficulties due to the sales slump. The two firms decided to merge and in 1931 they formed General Motors-Holden's Ltd, a company which continued to manufacture bodies for rival makes as well as assembling and eventually manufacturing cars of its own.

The body-making division ceased to make bodies for other vehicle manufacturers after WW2. The Holden car was launched in 1948.

1929 AAM

The AAM was the work of the Melbourne-based Australian Automotive Manufacturers Association.

Although the AAM was powered by a Chevrolet engine, all other parts, including the body, were manufactured by Association members. The prototype was exhibited at the 1929 Melbourne Motor Show. A few orders were taken but production did not proceed.

1933 BUCKINGHAM

The Buckingham car was advertised as an 'entirely new motor car designed and built in Australia by Australian workmen using Australian materials'.

It was produced by Buckingham & Ward (Australia) Ltd and first exhibited at the 1933 Melbourne Motor Show. Powered by a four-cylinder Australian-made engine rated at 22 HP, the car was built as a four-door sedan (Buckingham 60) and two-door coupe (Buckingham 70). The company purchased the engineering works of Humble & Sons in Geelong to give them the facilities for volume production. Meanwhile, the prototype was driven for almost 50 000 km on proving trials.

At about the same time, Buckingham & Ward announced a commercial vehicle to be called Ward. It failed but several Buckingham cars were sold before the company ceased production of all vehicles.

1933 SOUTHERN CROSS

Sir Charles Kingsford Smith was the greatest aviator of his day. If he had lived longer he may have also been remembered as a great car maker.

In 1931 'Smithy' joined a flying colleague, Jim Marks, in a car-building project. The unusual car they intended to build was based on the 1923 Marks-Moir which had been designed by Jim Mark's father. This unusual machine was built on the monocoque principle, using laminated timber to form a single-piece frame and body.

In June 1933 the updated car — now named after the history-making Fokker trimotor plane which Smithy had flown across the Pacific Ocean — made its debut at Mascot Aerodrome, Sydney.

The plan was to produce two Southern Cross models: an open tourer and the 'Airline', a closed version of the same car. Both were powered by a Sydney-made horizontally opposed four-cylinder engine. Six months after the Mascot launching, Smithy made a much-publicised run from Sydney to Melbourne in 15½ hours during which time the engine never stopped.

Kingsford Smith was in England in 1935, apparently trying to raise more funds for the car project. He attempted to smash the England-Australian air speed record on the way back. His plane — called *Lady Southern Cross* — disappeared while crossing the Bay of Bengal and Smithy and his copilot were never seen again.

At least four Southern Cross cars were built — two open tourers and two Airline sedans — before the project was wound up. Two of these cars used a novel Melbourne-built torque convertor which included some basic elements of the modern automatic transmission.

1933 SHIELS

The unusual Shiels was a pioneer front-wheel drive sports car.

Built in 1933 by Mr L. Shiels of the Melbourne-based Phoenix Motors Pty Ltd, the car was powered by a six-cylinder engine rated at 18 HP driving a front-mounted gearbox and final drive unit. A maximum speed of 120 km/h was claimed.

According to an article published in a 1933 edition of *The Australian Automobile Trade Journal*, the car was conceived in 1929.

'Mr Shiels', it said, 'decided that there was a demand for a light yet powerful front-wheel drive sports car, if it could be made at a reasonable price.

'Mr Shiels set out to build one. Piece by piece the various details were designed and assembled ... and today we see the result which measures up to all the designer wished for his first model.'

Mr Shiels had served an apprenticeship with Tarrant Motors in Melbourne and had worked for Hupmobile and Oaklands in the US during the 1920s.

When his own Shiels prototype was exhibited it attracted many favourable comments. However, for a reason not announced, production did not commence.

1935 EGAN

The attractive and well-built Egan deserved success but disappeared without a trace.

The car was the work of William Egan, who owned a Geelong sheet metal firm. Egan's firm built 8000 car bodies before the early 1930s when new car sales hit rock bottom as a result of the depression. With virtually no body-making work coming to him from major car companies, Egan sought to keep his factory busy with his own design.

The Egan prototype — a four-door sedan featuring the 'airflow' styling made popular by Chrysler — was displayed at the 1935 Melbourne Motor Show. It was powered by a US-built Lycoming six-cylinder engine (developing 64 kW) coupled to an imported three-speed synchromesh transmission. Bendix hydraulic brakes and a Moss steering box were also fitted.

The Egan body sat on a locally made X-type chassis frame and the standard of finish and interior appointments were said to be extremely high.

The new car was well received and many orders were taken but, for a reason not now known, only two Egan cars were built.

1936 'RICHARDS' CHRYSLER

The Adelaide-based T.J. Richards & Sons was a company which had started constructing horse-drawn carriages and became one of Australia's best-known motor vehicle body manufacturers. It was eventually absorbed into Chrysler Australia Ltd.

In 1936 the company fitted a Chrysler with Australia's first all-steel sedan body.

T.J. Richards was founded by Tobias Richards in 1885. By 1916 it had moved into motor vehicle coachbuilding and was producing bodies for a range of locally made and locally assembled vehicles. By 1925 the company (with headquarters at Keswick, near Adelaide) was using mechanical presses and assembly-line techniques. In 1928 Richards started producing bodies for Chrysler.

By 1935 the firm supplied all the Australian bodies for vehicles produced by the Chrysler Corporation. The newly formed Chrysler Dodge De Soto Distributors (Australia) Pty Ltd then purchased an interest in T.J. Richards & Sons Ltd. In 1936 the firm upstaged Holden's Motor Body Builders and other rivals by making Australia's first all-steel sedan body. Until then, locally made sedans had fabric panels (supported by concealed timber) in the roof because no company had a sufficiently large press to stamp out a complete turret roof.

T.J. Richards & Sons Ltd became Richards Industries in 1941. By this time the firm was mainly working on Dodge and other Chrysler vehicles. It became part of Chrysler Australia in 1951.

1938 AUSCAR

The Auscar was produced in 1938 by the Australian Car Syndicate.

The Syndicate's plan was to mass-produce the Auscar to sell for the equivalent of $500, less than the popular Fords and Vauxhalls of the day. The venture proceeded in the belief that the Federal Government would provide a bounty on locally made cars to conserve overseas funds.

The Auscar used a four-cylinder 15 HP engine which had been designed and built in South Australia. The complete car made its debut at the Royal Adelaide Show and, although some orders were taken, WW2 intervened and the project was discontinued.

1939 BATEUP

The low-priced Bateup car was a project launched by a group of Adelaide businessmen headed by car dealer George Bateup. The start of WW2 put an end to the project.

1944 DIECASTER

The Melbourne firm of Diecasters built a prototype car towards the end of WW2.

There was talk of mass production but nothing came of it.

1945 MCM

The MCM, conceived by Sydney speedway rider Jim McMahon in 1944-45, was one of the most promising attempts to produce an Australian car immediately after WW2.

But for McMahon's tragic death at the age of 35, it might have been a success.

In 1945 McMahon built a prototype open two-seater which had a wooden-framed steel body with a steeply sloping windscreen. The body was dated in style, with an 'alligator' bonnet and dicky seat, but the MCM was impressive mechanically.

The strong and simple design was developed with mass production in mind. It made use of a lightweight tubular steel chassis, had a high ground clearance and an unusual and innovative suspension system. A roller type accelerator was placed between the brake and clutch pedals.

A variety of components was employed, including some from a Morris 8/40. The prototype was powered by a modified two-cylinder DKW engine, fitted as a stopgap whilst McMahon developed his own. The engine intended for the MCM was an unorthodox design with a high power-to-weight ratio. It used a mixture of Ford V-8, Triumph motorbike and self-designed parts.

In July 1948 McMahon was in the US testing this engine in a midget racer. While on a banked track in California, he was thrashing all opposition when the throttle jammed open. The car ran into a fence and hit a stanchion, killing McMahon and ending the MCM project.

1948 GM-H HOLDEN 48-215

The Holden was Australia's first successful mass-produced car and became as much a part of the national culture as the proverbial 'football, meat pies and kangaroos'.

It came about largely due to the work of Larry (later Sir Laurence) Hartnett, a one-time director of General Motor's Vauxhall subsidiary, who came to Melbourne to work for General Motors-Holden's in the early 1930s.

At the end of WW2, Hartnett convinced the Federal Government that the country needed a car built in Australia for Australians. He persuaded his parent company to cooperate and the project began.

Hartnett had many disputes with his American counterparts, especially over the design of the car and the funding of the project. While these battles were taking place, some prototypes were built by a joint US/Australian team.

The new car was originally to be called the GM-H but a decision was made to call it Holden after the body-building company which had merged with GM Australia in the early 1930s.

In December 1946 Hartnett resigned from GM-H but the car project continued. The first Holden, designated the 48-215 and later commonly called the FX, was officially launched on 29 November 1948, by Prime Minister Chifley.

The Holden, which was 4.4 metres long and weighed 992 kg, was an advanced design with strong, lightweight unitary construction. It combined excellent performance and fuel economy. Power came from a 2.15-litre, six-cylinder 45 kW engine coupled to a three-speed column-shift manual gearbox. Maximum speed was about 130 km/h.

The Holden sold remarkably well. Even though the retail price rose by 33 per cent in less than two years, the number of buyers continued to exceed the output.

In January 1951 a coupe-utility was added to the range; in July 1953 a 'Business Sedan' (taxi version) appeared.

120 402 of the original 48-215s were built before the facelifted Holden FJ was released in October 1953.□

1896 Shearer steam carriage

1904 Ohlmeyer 'Jigger'

1906 Tarrant

1919 Australian Six

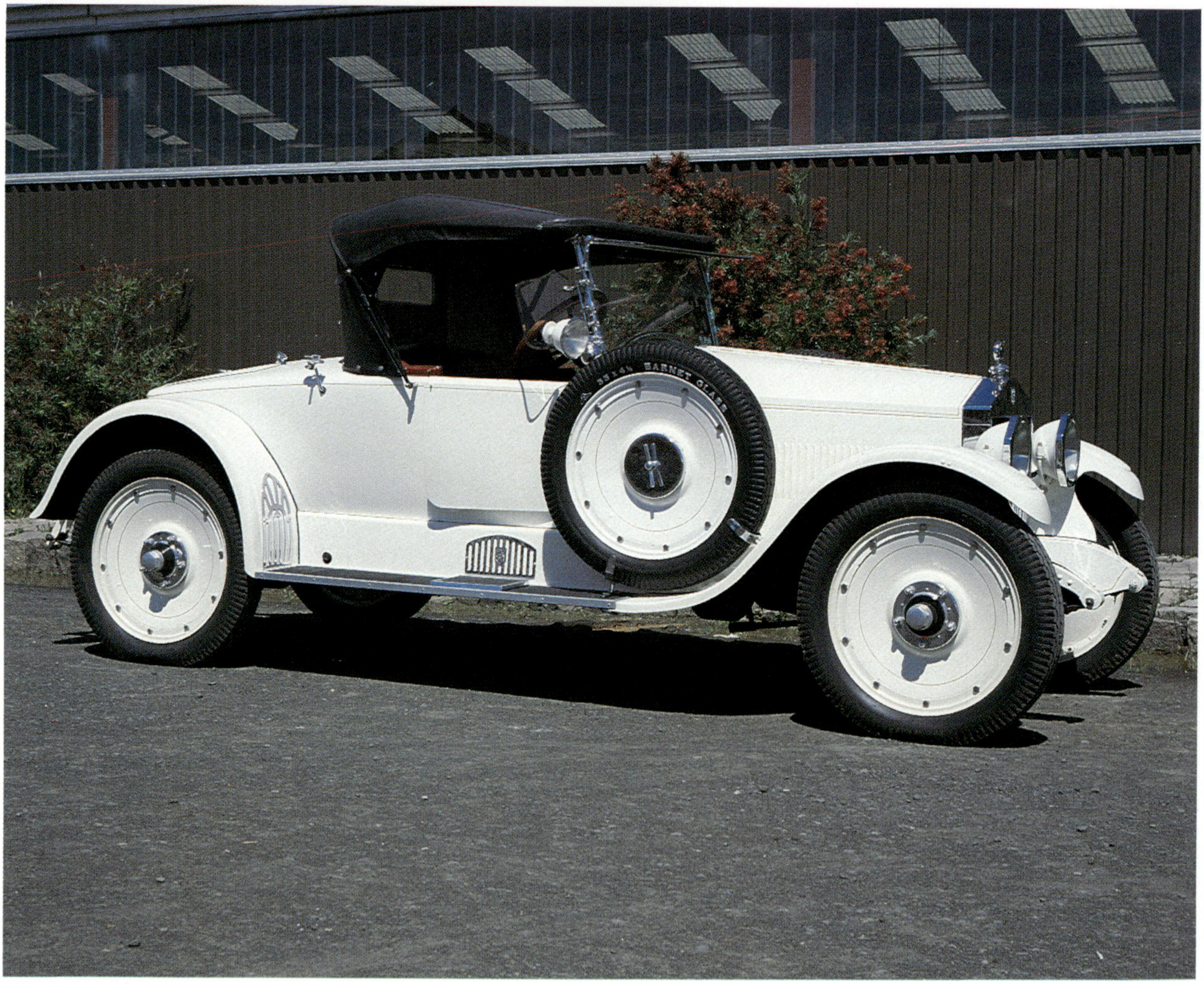

1919 Lincoln

1929 GMA Chevrolet Tourer (with Holden body)

1948 Holden 48-215

1958 Ascort

1970 Bolwell Nagari

1970 Valiant VG 'Hemi' Pacer

1970 Austin X6 Kimberly

1972 Valiant Charger R/T E49

1970 Falcon XY 'Shaker' GT

(courtesy Modern Motor magazine)

1949 HARTNETT

The Hartnett, produced in Melbourne from 1949 to 1955, is a small car with a fascinating history.

The main force behind it was Larry (later Sir Laurence) Hartnett, a leading motor industry figure whose colourful 60-year career included initiating the Holden project while chief executive of General Motors-Holden's.

After bailing out of GM-H, Hartnett decided to run his own car-making business. He selected a front-wheel drive, four-seater British car designed by Frenchman Jean Gregoire and purchased the manufacturing rights.

When first put on display in Australia (as the Hartnett) in 1949, the new car attracted 2000 firm orders. It featured independent suspension on all wheels, rack-and-pinion steering and a 600 mL, horizontally opposed, two-cylinder engine which was aircooled.

Plans to sell 10 000 cars a year were announced but Hartnett quickly ran into major problems. Offers from the Victorian Government to make a large loan and provide a rent-free factory were withdrawn and all the established body-making companies — including Holden's — declined to produce the body.

To raise money, Hartnett floated a public company. He leased a factory and arranged for Commonwealth Engineering — a firm with no previous body-building experience — to produce the metal panels. Within months 120 rolling chassis had been completed but not one body panel had been delivered.

Hartnett sued the supplier and eventually won the case with costs. The legal battle, however, had lasted for four and a half years, by which time the car-making project was beyond revival.

Hartnett was later to claim that there had been a carefully organised effort to prevent him from succeeding. He did not give up, however. His next attempt to launch an Australian car was the Lloyd-Hartnett, first sold in 1957. □

1949 WILES

One of several vehicles planned for mass production immediately after WW2, the small Wiles appeared in 1949.

The prototype, possibly based on a pre-WW2 DKW model, had a two-cylinder, two-stroke engine rated at 7 HP. It was designed by a Captain Jack Thompson and built by the Wiles Manufacturing Company of Adelaide.

The intention was to produce an inexpensive 'people's car' offering basic motoring without frills. Good fuel consumption and a top speed of 80 km/h were claimed.

Production did not proceed.

1949 JB MINOR

The unusual JB Minor minicar was designed and built in Northgate, Queensland.

The initials stood for its makers, Jeffress Brothers. The JB Minor was powered by a two-stroke 5 HP engine driving the front wheels through a hydraulic transmission. Steering was effected by turning the rear wheels. Though the prototype was publicly displayed in 1949, production never commenced.

1950 REVILLE RANGER

Named after, and promoted by, speedway driver Jean Reville, the Reville Ranger was a Jeep/Land Rover-type vehicle.

It was designed to offer buyers a large variety of body styles and mechanical specifications. The Queensland-based Reville Motor Company published illustrations of the Ranger but it is not known if any were built.

1950 BASSIN

Another Sydney car-making project which never took off, the Bassin was advertised but it is doubtful if more than a primitive prototype was built.

The production version of the Bassin was to have a laminated wooden body and a choice between 10 HP and 12 HP horizontally opposed engines.

1953 GM-H HOLDEN FJ

Holden number two — the famous FJ model — was launched in October 1953.

Despite the near-legendary status now attached to this car, it was little more than a facelifted and updated version of the original 48-215 design. It used an identical engine and gearbox, but a more robust rear axle.

Some FJ mechanical changes, including the replacement of the lever-action shock absorbers with a more durable telescopic type, had been incorporated in the later series 48-215s. The FJ introduced an adjustable differential.

The main styling changes were a new grille, different hubcaps and bumpers plus several chrome body mouldings.

Three FJ sedan types were produced — Special, Standard and Business — with coupe-utility and panel van body styles also available. A wagon prototype was constructed but, as GM-H couldn't keep up with demand for the sedan and light commercial models, it was not put into production.

The FJ offered a much greater list of options that its predecessor and was available in 12 colours. The Special model featured armrests and a cigarette lighter. It was available in a two-tone finish.

A 1952 expansion plan costing $11 million was aimed at lifting production from 85 to 200 units per day.

The FJ was the first Holden to be exported, with small numbers going to New Zealand from 1954.

GM-H built a total of 169 969 FJs in three years. □

1953 TILBROOKS

The three-wheeler Tilbrooks car was built by the Tilbrooks company of Kensington, South Australia.

The company — primarily a producer of motorcycles and sidecars — designed, built and displayed the prototype three-wheeler in 1953. A 197 mL Villiers engine and independent front suspension were fitted. Production plans did not proceed.

1955 EDITH

The Edith three-wheeler was claimed to be the first minicar to go into local production.

The engineering firm of Gray & Harper Pty Ltd had designed the small car at Huntingdale in Victoria around 1952. Small scale production started three years later.

Powered by a 197 mL Villiers two-stroke engine driving the single rear wheel, the prototype Edith was designed as an alternative to the European bubble cars (such as the Messerschmitt) then on local sale. It was intended to sell the Edith for half the cost of a new Holden but only a few were made.

1955 TONTALA

The Tontala Motor Company was established in Canterbury, Victoria, in the early 1950s to construct fibreglass-bodied sports cars.

The firm displayed a prototype two-door sports coupe at the 1955 Melbourne Motor Show. This was based entirely on Holden mechanical components with a European-style body. The company took out advertisements in magazines offering assemble-at-home Tontala kits. Few, if any, were sold.

1956 BUCKLE

The unusual-looking Buckle GT Tourer was a fibreglass two-plus-two coupe designed, built and marketed by Bill Buckle of Sydney.

Produced from 1956 to early 1960, it employed a Ford Zephyr six-cylinder engine and other mass-produced mechanical components.

The coupe body sat on a box chassis frame with a transverse leaf spring front suspension and conventional Ford rear axle. It weighed only 865 kg and had a top speed of 160 km/h. The design incorporated fold-down rear seats, an adjustable steering column and electrically operated door locks — unusual features for the era.

Initial sales of the Buckle coupes, priced at the then high figure of 1700 pounds ($3400), were promising and Buckle entered his cars in motor sport events to further boost interest.

Buckle himself raced one of his coupes for three years, improving it continually and achieving impressive results in hillclimbs and circuit racing. Unfortunately, success on the racetrack didn't equal financial success. Production of the Buckle ceased in 1960, by which time a large amount of money had been lost. Bill Buckle later turned the tables, however, with the Australian/German Goggomobil and became one of the few Australians ever to operate a profitable car-making business.

A total of 25 Buckle cars was made, including the 1955 prototype which was even more unusual in styling than the production model.

1956 GM-H HOLDEN FE

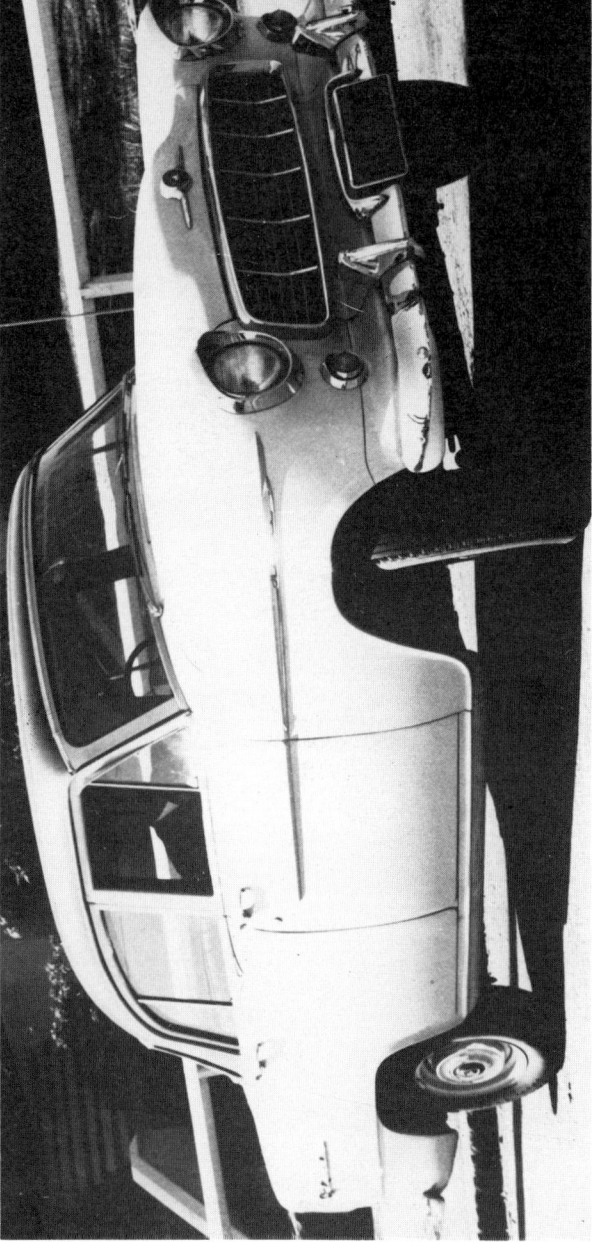

The Holden FE, released July 1956, was the first Holden totally developed in Australia.

It replaced the highly successful 48-215/FJ series and introduced a completely new body.

More modern in appearance than its predecessor, the FE was heavily influenced by the Chevrolet and Opel models of the day. It had a longer wheelbase and wider track than the 48-215/FJ design and was lower. A flatter bonnet and boot accentuated its length.

A one-piece curved windscreen replaced the previous two-piece flat glass screen. A larger rear window further increased the glass area and the new model offered 40 per cent more visibility.

Although the original Holden drivetrain was carried over, engine power was slightly increased by lifting the engine compression ratio and using stiffened head pistons and larger valves. A 12 volt electrical system was fitted for the first time.

The FE had redesigned steering and front suspension units and a hydraulically operated clutch. It ran on smaller 33 cm (13 inch) wheels and was initially available in three versions, Standard, Special and Business sedans.

Many new colour schemes were available including two-tone finishes. Some stainless steel mouldings were used on the bodywork in place of chrome plating. The interior room was increased and a new instrument panel incorporated a lockable glove box.

The first Holden station wagon was released shortly after the rest of the FE range.

Today the FE might look like a humble motor car, but in the 1950s it was considered by many to be a finely sculptured work of art. In the September 1956 edition of *Modern Motor* magazine, a journalist explained how, after parking the FE he was testing on the street, he had to fight through an admiring crowd to get back to it.

The FE had a production run of 155 161 units.

1957 MORRIS MARSHALL

The Morris Marshall, complete with a a boomerang motif on the grille, was BMC Australia's tentative test of the six-cylinder market.

It was one of many Morris models assembled and partly manufactured in Australia. All were derived from British designs but were claimed to be 'adapted for Australian conditions'.

The Marshall was a modified Austin A95 Westminster. Powered by a 2.64-litre engine coupled to a four-speed gearbox, it was a four-door saloon which could seat five or six. First sold in 1957, it was less than a sales success. Morris, for example, sold 11,626 cars in 1959, comprising 4471 Minor 1000s, 6776 Majors and only 379 Marshalls.

The Marshall continued unchanged until June 1960, when it was dropped from the BMC line-up.

1957 TILLI CAPTON

The Tilli Capton, a three-wheeler car produced in Melbourne, was intended to be the cheapest car on the market.

It appeared in 1957, powered by a two-cylinder, two-stroke Anzani engine rated at 15 HP. The fibreglass body was unusually styled (read ugly!), had a fixed hardtop and recessed headlights and could seat two or three people.

Plans were announced to volume-produce the low-budget car at the rate of 200 per month. The project was halted, however, at an early stage, with no reasons being given.

1957 LLOYD-HARTNETT

After the failure of the Hartnett car in the mid-1950s, the dynamic Larry (later Sir Laurence) Hartnett announced a new venture.

It was the Lloyd-Hartnett, an Australian version of the Lloyd 600, an unusual German front-wheel drive minicar.

The plan was to initially assemble the car in a new plant at Brisbane and progressively introduce locally-made components as the volume increased.

The Lloyd-Hartnett went on sale in December 1957. Powered by an aircooled, 600 mL, two-cylinder engine, it proved a lively and practical vehicle. The all-steel body, mounted on a backbone chassis, seated four people. The luggage compartment could be extended by folding down the rear seat — an innovative idea at the time.

The design provided exceptional fuel economy. Running at speeds of 90 to 100 km/h, one Lloyd-Hartnett averaged 4.6 litres per 100 kilometres between Sydney and Melbourne. The petrol cost was the equivalent of $3.40.

Just when the Lloyd-Hartnett was beginning to gain a sound reputation, the German company closed down. The Australian operation, with its supply of components stopped, was also soon forced to shut. The last Lloyd-Hartnetts were built in 1962. A total of 3000 had been sold.

Laurence Hartnett then started importing Datsun cars from Japan. In the mid-1960s he proposed a plan to fully manufacture a new six-cylinder Nissan/Datsun design in Australia but could not get Federal Government permission.

Hartnett worked on a string of varied projects until his death in 1986.

1958 ASCORT

The fibreglass Ascort coupe was one of the earliest and most classy local attempts to turn the humble VW Beetle into an excitement machine.

Built in Sydney by Mirek Craney from 1958, the Ascort was based on a Volkswagen chassis with the standard 1.2-litre engine modified to produce 41 kW. The locally made four-seater body had double skins for strength and was well appointed and trimmed. Extensive sound-deadening material was employed. A first-aid kit within the front armrest was one of several novel interior features.

With its light body, the Ascort weighed 33 per cent less than a standard Beetle. Top speed was 144 km/h.

More than a dozen Ascorts were built before the project collapsed. □

1958 GM-H HOLDEN FC

The FC was released at a time when half of all the cars sold in Australia were Holdens.

The new model, which replaced the FE in May 1958, had mildly revised styling which included a bolder grille, ornamental chrome fins and body side mouldings.

Mechanically there was little change. The original 'grey' engine (named after the painted block) was retained but its torque qualities were improved by the fitting of an improved camshaft. There were also minor improvements to the suspension, brakes, gear-change linkages and steering box.

Redesigned interior trim was supplemented by a new steering wheel and an improved driver seating position.

The seven FC models included a utility, panel van and two versions of the Station Sedan wagon.

The FC outsold the FE, with a production run of 191 724 units in 20 months. Meanwhile the company's share of the booming market for new vehicles had risen from 20.7 per cent in 1950 to an astounding 50.3 per cent in 1958. It was outselling its nearest rival two to one.

During the FC production run, the 500 000th Holden was produced and the 10 000th Holden was exported.

The phenomenal success of the Holden was attracting big interest overseas. In 1959 the English *Motor* magazine conducted a special roadtest of an FC which had been exported to the UK. They remarked:

'It is not ornate or glamorous but after a thousand miles we were immensely appreciative of its solid worth as a roomy, comfortable and smoothly easy-going sort of car which seemed sturdy and certainly did not cost a lot to run.'

1958 GOGGOMOBIL DART

The Goggomobil was a hybrid German-Australian car built in Australia between 1958 and 1961.

The project was launched in Sydney by Bill Buckle who had earlier built and sold his own design, the Buckle coupe.

For the Goggomobil, Buckle secured the rights to a small car made by Hans Glas of Dingolfing, Bavaria.

The German product had an all-steel body but Buckle fitted his cars with fibreglass bodies. He offered three body styles — sedan, coupe and open two-seater.

The open version — known as the Dart — was Buckle's own design but, like the sedan and coupe, it used imported Goggomobil components. No doors were fitted but the sides were so low the occupants could step over them. A minute 300 mL two-cylinder engine was located in the rear, a small luggage compartment was built into the nose.

The Dart weighed only 345 kg and was powered by a 13 kW engine. The maximum road speed was only about 90 km/h but, because of its low gearing, the tiny sports car was capable of remarkable acceleration. Once described as looking like 'an eggshell on wheels', it is now keenly sought by collectors.

Buckle sold a total of 5000 Goggomobil sedans, coupes and Darts before 1961, when the Mini Minor arrived in Australia. The Mini was more modern and powerful but sold at virtually the same price, thereby spelling the end for the Goggomobil.

Unlike the Buckle and almost every other Australian car of this type, the Goggomobil was a profitable enterprise.

1958 AUSTIN LANCER

Although Austin models were first assembled and partly manufactured in Australia before WW1, the 1958 Lancer was probably the first to have a significant local design input.

The Lancer was one of 'twins' produced by BMC in Australia, the other being the Morris Major.

Powered by a 1.5-litre, four-cylinder engine, the Lancer (like the Major) was based largely on the Wolseley 1500. By the standards of the day, the Lancer had an above average power-to-weight ratio. It was praised for its brisk acceleration and top speed of 125 km/h, which was considered impressive for a small car.

Despite the car's virtues, Lancer sales were slow and the model was dropped in favour of the locally assembled British A40 Farina.

The line between what is Australian and what is not becomes particularly blurred with BMC/Leyland cars, which were produced in almost infinite variations wearing a variety of badges in dozens of countries.

Other post-WW2 Austins assembled in Australia and 'adapted for local conditions' include the Austin A30 (1952-56), A50 Cambridge (1954-56), A55 (1957-59), A40 Farina (1959-62), A60 (1959-62), A60 Countryman wagon (1960-62), the six-cylinder A90/95/99 (1955-60) and the A105 Westminster (1957-59).

1958 BUCHANAN COBRA

Combining eye-catching styling, excellent design and a low purchase price, the Buchanan Cobra looked to have everything needed for success. But, sadly, it joined the long list of Australian automotive failures.

The Cobra was designed and built by Nat Buchanan of Sydney, who had started in the car-making business by producing fibreglass bodies to fit sports car chassis. In 1956 he sold a self-designed fibreglass shell with styling influenced by the Aston Martin DB3S. This low-cost body converted the 'square-rigger' MG TC/TD to a sleek, streamlined 'racer' and 35 were sold in the first six months of production.

Aided by publicity derived from a string of motor sport victories by Buchanan-bodied cars (including first place in the Queensland Hillclimb Championship), the company had sold 80 bodies by mid-1958.

In that year, Buchanan launched the Cobra, a complete sporting two-seater car fitted with a fibreglass body and box section chassis. Although the engine was a four-cylinder 28 kW unit taken from the unexciting Standard Ten sedan, it gave good performance when put in the lightweight Cobra. Top speed was around 130 km/h.

The Cobra also boasted a high-quality body finish, a large boot, wind-up windows, high ground clearance and other features not normally found in sports cars of the day. Plans were made for volume production to start in January 1959, with sales being handled through Standard-Triumph dealers. A mere seven Cobras were built and sold before the distribution plans were cancelled and Nat Buchanan withdrew from car production.

1960 GM-H HOLDEN FB

To answer the forthcoming Ford Falcon, GM-H replaced the Holden FC with the FB model in January 1960.

Essentially a revised version of the previous Holden FC, this new model was advertised as being longer, roomier, heavier, lower and more powerful, although in every case it was only slightly so.

Styling changes included a lower bonnet line, finned rear guards and new tail-lights. The wheelbase remained the same but the length was increased by 14 cm. A wraparound windscreen mimicked the big US trend of the mid-to-late 1950s.

The previous six-cylinder engine block was bored, giving it a slightly larger capacity of 2.26 litres. The compression ratio was raised and the output was lifted to just over 56 kW.

The FB had improved seating (giving slightly increased passenger room) and was the first Holden with acrylic paintwork (replacing the old nitrocellulose 'Duco'). Upgraded brakes, heavier front coil springs, a dry element air cleaner and a new clutch were fitted. The instrument panel was completely changed but no new instruments were added.

The FB range included a Special sedan, Standard sedan, Special station wagon, Standard station wagon, utility and panel van.

The FB was the fifth new Holden in 11 years and enabled GM-H to maintain its amazing 50 per cent share of the Australian market. The FB was the first Holden to be produced in a left-hand drive version for export to Asian and Pacific countries.

A total of 174 747 FB Holdens was sold.

1960 FORD FALCON XK

By the early 1980s, the Falcon was Australia's most popular car. But Ford Australia's entry into the family car market nearly didn't make it past its second year.

The story started in the early 1950s when General Motors-Holden's was taking the lion's share of local car sales. Ford Australia officials knew they had to do something and in 1955 they decided to produce their own car. It was based on a new Ford 'compact' called Falcon which was being made ready for the US market.

Ford spent $30 million on the project before the first model, the Falcon XK sedan, was launched. It appeared in September 1960 with a 2.4-litre, six-cylinder OHV engine developing 67 kW at 4200 rpm. Transmission choice was a three-speed manual gearbox or a two-speed aircooled 'Fordomatic' automatic transmission.

Low-slung and fitted with an unusual five-bar concave grille, Falcon was widely considered the best looking local car on the market. Nevertheless, it proved fragile on rough roads and Ford was soon faced with a vast number of major warranty claims as well as the problem of strengthening the design.

The cost was so high that it was rumoured Ford would discontinue local production. However, aided by considerable support from the US company, Ford Australia persevered. The design continued to be improved and adapted for local conditions and, within a few years, it had little in common with the US design.

Following the release of the original XK sedan, Standard and Deluxe station wagons joined the range in November 1960. In May 1961 a utility version was released. A total of 68 465 XK Falcons was built.

1961 'CLAYTON' VOLKSWAGEN BEETLE

The famous VW 'People's Car' dates back to 1933 when German Chancellor Adolf Hitler commissioned Dr Ferdinand Porsche to create a small, low-priced car.

Three decades later the 'Beetle', as it became known, was manufactured in Australia at Clayton, Victoria.

The first Volkswagen was seen here in 1946 but it was not until 1953 that the Beetle was officially imported. Local assembly commenced in 1954. In 1957 the German factory joined with various State distributors and formed Volkswagen Australasia Ltd.

Meanwhile the rugged rear-engined two-door Beetle, powered by a small aircooled, horizontally opposed engine, was establishing an unbeatable record in Australian long-distance trials and rallies.

In the REDeX Round-Australia Trial of 1955, VWs came home first and second. In the 1956 Mobilgas Trial, VWs won six of the first ten places and in the 1957 Mobilgas Trial they managed a 1-2-3-4-5-6 finish.

With 'Beetlemania' at fever pitch, the first local sheet metal panels were produced in 1960. By 1967 the engine and most other parts were made at Clayton, and VWA was close to its objective of 95 per cent local content.

VWA had budgeted to produce 50 000 Beetles per year but even in their best year, 1964, they produced only 25 736. More modern competitors and rising prices gave the Beetle a pounding in the marketplace. Sales dropped to a mere 11 000 units in 1968, causing substantial losses and prompting the company to close the manufacturing operation and revert to local assembly. $20 million had been lost and the 'Australian' VW was finished.

In 1976 VWA's Clayton factory was sold to Nissan and local assembly of Volkswagens ceased. By then over 335 000 VWs had been sold in Australia.

The last Beetle was imported in May 1977.□

1961 GM-H HOLDEN EK

The Holden EK, a minor facelift of the FB, made its debut in May 1961.

It was introduced as a stopgap until the much more modern-looking EJ model was readied for release.

The EK's only significant mechanical change was the introduction of Holden's first automatic transmission.

By now the Falcon — released in 1960 — accounted for about 12.5 per cent of the sedan market, partly because it was available with a two-speed automatic transmission. GM-H was forced to match this feature on the Holden and decided to go one better and offer a three-speed.

The Holden unit, called the Hydra-Matic, was imported from Detroit but plans were announced for it to be fully manufactured in Australia. It was a much-praised unit and allowed the automatic Holden to maintain performance figures fairly close to those of the manual. Top speed was down only about 3 km/h and 0-100 km/h acceleration was about 2½ seconds slower.

The EK was identified by a new grille with wider spaced parking lights/flashers.

Refinements included revised interior trim, an electric wiper motor (replacing the vacuum unit), a new fresh-air heating unit and a bonnet lock.

The range of six Holden models continued, with buyers having a choice from two sedans, two station wagons, a panel van and a coupe-utility. The basic price was unchanged.

The EK stayed in production just over a year before the EJ model was introduced. Sales of the EK were hampered slightly by a credit squeeze but 150 214 were built. □

1962 CHRYSLER VALIANT R SERIES

The R Series Valiant was a sensation — a family sedan which could almost touch 100 mph (161 km/h) and run the standing quarter mile in well under 19 seconds.

Despite its foreign antecedents (the R Series was assembled from US parts), the Valiant incorporated modifications for Australia. And within ten years the marque would be wholly made in Australia and bear no resemblance to US models.

Local planning on the Valiant started in early 1961. To gain a marketing edge over Holden and Falcon, Chrysler Australia opted for the bigger of two engines offered with the car in the US. This was a 3.69-litre overhead-valve, six-cylinder unit inclined at 30 degrees to the right.

Called the '225' or 'Slant Six', the engine produced 109 kW — almost twice that of the 'Grey' motor of the 1962 Holden EK.

The newcomer set the stage for a heated three-way sales battle that would last all the 1960s and well into the 1970s. It also started a power 'war'.

The Valiant came in just one body style — a four-door sedan. It had a three-speed gearbox with a floor-mounted gearlever; a push-button three-speed automatic transmission was optional. Seats were of the bench type and instrumentation was pretty basic. A fake spare tyre mount graced the boot lid.

The most pleasing things about the Valiant were its looks, size and power. The press described its low-slung body styling as 'space age' and its power as 'exceptional'. Buyers were so keen that the first batch of 1008 R Series Valiants sold out in days. By that time, Chrysler Australia had imported sufficient parts to start assembling the later model S Series Valiant.

1962 GM-H HOLDEN EJ PREMIER

After Chrysler launched the highly acclaimed R Series Valiant, GM-H countered with the Holden EJ, using a completely new body.

The EJ Holden looked a much more modern car than its predecessor (the EK), having a lower profile, a flatter bonnet and a squarer rear end.

In spite of being lower, the Holden's traditional high ground clearance was maintained and there was still plenty of headroom. The wagon had a rear cargo tray well over two metres long.

The previous Holden drive train was carried over but there were mechanical improvements including new Duo Servo brakes and a strengthened front suspension. An improved Hydra-Matic transmission — which GM-H described as 'similar to the unit used in Cadillac and Oldsmobile' — was available on all models.

The EJ was first tested in November 1960 and GM-H claimed it was subjected to the most exhaustive testing ever done on an Australian car.

This model range brought about the introduction of the upmarket Premier sedan. The first Premier, now a collectors' item, used the same body and drive train as other models but featured leather-covered bucket seats, a heater, wool pile carpet, whitewall tyres, a floor console and other luxury features. It had some additional body ornamentation and was the first Holden with metallic paint.

The EJ proved slightly more popular than the EK, with 154 811 built, including the millionth Holden.

1962 AUSTIN FREEWAY

The Austin Freeway represented the first of BMC/Leyland's three attempts to burst into the Holden/Falcon/Valiant market with a locally designed and built car.

Slightly dearer than the competition, the six-cylinder Freeway was lavishly equipped by the standards of the day with windscreen washers, a fresh-air heater/demister unit and other features not standard on most other cars.

It was available in sedan and wagon form and was advertised as being 'Made For and By Australians'.

Loosely based on the styling of the Farina A60, the Freeway was powered by a unique, locally built 2.4-litre engine. A Wolseley version of the same car was also made.

The Freeway and Wolseley were released at a time when BMC's fortunes were soaring on the back of the Mini Minor, which had been assembled and partly manufactured at Zetland (Sydney) from March 1961.

For the next few years the company's sales would go from strength to strength in the small-car field but hopes that this success would carry over to the full-size family car market were not realised. Only 3090 Freeways were sold in the first year, even fewer in 1963. Production was discontinued in 1965.

1962 CHRYSLER VALIANT S SERIES

The S Series Valiant was rushed to the showroom floor when a stampede of customers cleared Chrysler Australia's entire stock of the earlier R Series.

The Valiant was intended as Chrysler Australia's answer to the big-selling Holden and Falcon and, with a large scale importation of S Series parts, Chrysler for the first time was able to produce the Valiant in volume.

The S Series was a minor refinement of the previous model. Like its predecessor, it was a locally assembled US design and was offered to the Australian public in only one form — a four-door sedan.

Changes were minimal, the most obvious being the revised grille and the removal of the fake spare tyre mount from the rear boot lid.

Other differences included round tail-lights, a steering-column gearshift (replacing the floor lever), a greater braking area, a larger fuel tank and a corrosion-resistant exhaust muffler.

The new model was slightly dearer than the old, but few buyers, if any, were deterred. The waiting list was still very long and, by May 1963 (when the replacement AP5 model was released), 10 009 S Series Valiants had been made.□

1962 FORD FALCON XL

In August 1962 Ford Australia facelifted the original 1960 XK Falcon and introduced new features and new luxury models.

The updated XL version had 734 new parts including a new gearbox, clutch, starter motor, air cleaner and suspension system. A new carburettor was said to greatly improve fuel economy and an engine vibration damper reduced interior noise at speed.

The XL featured a convex grille, revised tail-lights and bumper-mounted front park/turn signals. The squared-off flat roof had swept-back rear pillars and was described by Ford as a 'Thunderbird roofline'.

In October 1962 the more powerful 75 kW Pursuit engine became available as an option.

The XL range was widened with the release of the Squire, a deluxe version of the station wagon. The Futura — a luxury sedan — followed.

Including the utility and 'sedan delivery van' versions, Falcon was now available in ten models. And Ford was offering one of the widest range of accessories available with any car in Australia. Aside from such rarities (for 1962) as a factory-approved roof-rack, there were dust deflectors (for the wagon), instrument panel safety padding, trouble lights and even an electric shaver!

Falcon sales received a valuable boost when an XL was driven to victory in the 1962 Armstrong 500 at Phillip Island. This was the first of a long string of Falcon motor sport victories.

75 765 XL Falcons were built.

1963 ZETA SALOON

The unorthodox-looking Zeta saloon was a multipurpose family car using a mixture of locally made and imported parts.

Produced in Adelaide by Lightburn & Company Ltd from 1963, it was made in small numbers until 1966.

The Zeta was claimed to be the first vehicle sold in Australia which combined the attributes of a sedan, wagon and light delivery truck. Its two-door fibreglass body was an ungainly but ingenious design with seats which could be folded flat or quickly removed to provide a large cargo area. The seats could also be fitted to the roof to provide a grandstand view for sporting events!

The low-priced four-passenger car weighed only 436 kg. Power came from a Villiers 324 mL two-stroke engine driving the front wheels through a Burman motorcycle gearbox. The wheelbase was 1.88 metres. Handling was nervous at best.

In 1964 a two-seater Zeta sports car was also built by Lightburn. Harold Lightburn, whose main business was producing car jacks, concrete-mixers and power tools, announced ambitious plans to build 50 Zeta cars a week but only 363 were made over a three-year period.

1963 CHRYSLER VALIANT AP5

In 1962 Chrysler had found instant and formidable success with its US-built/Australian-assembled Valiant. Company officials were determined to consolidate this success with a car made in Australia for Australians.

The 'Aussie Valiant', designated the 'AP5', replaced the S Series in May of 1963. Although based on the US Valiant (like its two predecessors), it was considerably modified for local conditions and shared only six body panels with its American counterpart.

The AP5 introduced a completely new — and more conventional — appearance. It was of a similar width to the previous model but slightly longer.

The AP5 used the same 3.6-litre 'Slant Six' 225 engine as previous models but had a new single-barrel, downdraft Holley carburettor which retained the 109 kW output while slightly improving fuel economy. The engines were still imported, as were some outer body panels.

The AP5 had only two headlights instead of the previous model's four. The interior trim was a two-tone synthetic material. 'Extras' such as sun visors, cigar lighters and ashtrays topped a fairly modest standard equipment list.

A special version — the Valiant Regal — was released to compete with the luxury Holden Premier and Falcon Futura.

The Regal had more body decoration than the standard Valiant, better seats, automatic transmission and other features. It was identified by bonnet and boot emblems, whitewall tyres and distinctive wheel trims.

In November 1963 'Safari' station wagon variants were added to the range in manual, automatic and Regal form.

A total of 49 440 AP5 Valiants was built.□

1963 GM-H HOLDEN EH

In August 1963 the eighth model Holden, the EH, was announced. Over the next 18 months, a record 256 959 were sold.

Although it was only a facelifted EJ, the styling work was very effective and, with the addition of some retooled panels and a new-look roofline, the new model offered a significantly more modern appearance.

The EH series was powered by two versions of a completely new six-cylinder engine, the 149 and 179 (named after their cubic inch sizes), respectively 2.45 and 2.95 litres in capacity. This engine was dubbed the 'red motor', after the colour of the painted block, to distinguish it from the long-in-the-tooth grey-coloured engine used in all previous Holdens.

The 149, fitted as standard to all models except the luxury Premier, was 33 per cent more powerful than the 'grey' engine, the 179 was 53 per cent more powerful. A low-compression version of the 149 was also available.

GM-H boasted that its engine plant — which delivered a completed engine every 1½ minutes — was the most modern in the world.

The EH range was expanded with a wagon version of the Premier. This, like the Premier sedan, featured Hydra-Matic automatic transmission, front bucket seats, leather trim and wool pile carpets.

Despite all the new features, the EH sold for the same price as the EJ it replaced. The standard sedan was actually 55 pounds ($110) cheaper than the equivalent 1952 model in a time when the average wage was much higher. It's little wonder GM-H was soon selling more than 14 000 Holden EHs every month.

GM-H meanwhile, was expanding in every direction as 1964 turned into a boom year. The EH 'S4' (with upgraded brakes, a bigger fuel tank and other minor modifications) was raced at Bathurst in 1964. Although its results were unspectacular, this outing was a precursor to 'The General's' later dominance on the mountain circuit.

1964 FORD FALCON XM HARDTOP

By 1964 the Australian market was getting so competitive that prices were actually being reduced.

When Ford announced its new XM Falcon in February 1964 there was a price cut of 14 pounds ($28).

The XM was another local facelift of the original XK model. Buyers now had a choice of three six-cylinder engines — 2.4, 2.8 and 3.3 litres — supplemented by a 90 kW 'Super Pursuit Six' version of the 3.3.

Styling changes were mainly cosmetic and included moving the circular tail-lights to the top of the boot line and the fitting of a chrome surround to the front grille. A dummy air-scoop was fitted and the word 'Ford' spelled out across the bonnet.

The Futura was upgraded with the Pursuit engine and whitewall tyres fitted as standard equipment. The Squire wagon came with a padded dashboard and a power-operated tailgate window.

The two-speed watercooled Fordomatic transmission became available on all engines in the Falcon XM passenger car range.

In July 1964 the two-door Falcon was released. This pillarless coupe was sold in Deluxe Hardtop and Futura Hardtop forms. As standard equipment, the Futura Hardtop boasted bucket seats and, according to the brochure, a 'Million Pound Ride'.

47 039 XMs were sold.

1964 ZETA SPORTS

The tiny Italian-styled Zeta Sports was built by the Adelaide-based Lightburn & Company Ltd.

After introducing the Zeta saloon in 1963, Lightburn followed with the rear-engined Michelotti-designed Sports model.

It was powered by a 500 mL two-stroke engine made by the German FMR company. The engine developed 16 kW, giving the Zeta a claimed top speed of 120 km/h.

The Sports had two seats mounted in a fibreglass body sitting on a tubular chassis. The wheelbase was 1.9 metres.

Only 48 Zeta Sports were made, compared with just over 300 saloons. The Lightburn company ceased making cars in 1966.

1965 GM-H HOLDEN HD

The Holden HD range arrived in February 1965 with a restyled body, Powerglide automatic transmission and the most powerful Holden engine yet released.

The body styling was up to date with US trends, which in the 1960s were the benchmark for automotive design. The HD was wider and five centimetres longer than the EH model it replaced and offered substantial increases in passenger and load space.

Equipment levels were higher and self-adjusting brakes were fitted as standard.

The HD introduced the high-performance X2 engine, which was fitted with twin Bendix carburettors, a modified camshaft, new inlet and exhaust manifolds and a low-restriction exhaust system. This engine developed 105 kW, 19 kW up on standard, and was available as an option for all models.

The HD offered the Holden buyer the greatest choice of variants yet. He or she could choose from three engines and two gearboxes. The comparatively large list of options included disc brakes and a vinyl roof.

Initially the HD was available as a sedan and station wagon, but a utility and panel van followed.

Unfortunately the HD release was followed by a downturn in the market. Although initial sales figures were very high, they soon slowed dramatically.

Strangely, many people thought that the HD's body design was too unusual. The press criticised its sharp-edged front guards, and cited them as a danger to pedestrians.

178 927 HD Holdens were built.□

1965 FORD FALCON XP

In March 1965 the original Falcon body was updated for the last time and the Fairmont luxury variant was released.

The XP's body changes included slab-sided styling, 'eyebrows' on the front guards and a new grille with 11 vertical bars. The XP bonnet was 80 mm longer than the XM bonnet, and the car featured a restyled 'squared off' look.

The new Falcon offered a three-speed automatic which Ford said was the first to be developed and manufactured in Australia.

The Fairmont made its debut in sedan and wagon forms. This prestige Falcon replaced the Futura sedan and Squire wagon but the Futura two-door was continued. The Fairmont was Ford's attempt to counter Holden's Premier and Valiant's Regal and V-8. It used the same body shell as the XP Falcon with minor brightwork changes and distinctive badging.

The Fairmont had fully adjustable front bucket seats, a 3.3-litre 'Super Pursuit Six' engine, three-speed automatic transmission, front-wheel disc brakes, low-profile tyres, two-speed heater-demister and a more luxurious trim. Ford didn't follow Chrysler, however, and incorporate the latest and greatest US feature — a vinyl roof.

Despite the lack of major changes, *Wheels* magazine called the XP 'the best Falcon yet'. They said the new model was more solid, more refined and better looking than its predecessor. 'It has now reached the stage where it can meet its opposition toe-to-toe and not come out the underdog', the magazine said.

The XP sold well with 70 998 built.

1965 CHRYSLER VALIANT AP6 V-8

When Chrysler revised the AP5 Valiant in March 1965, the company decided to leave the best till last.

It was to be several months before the sensational AP6 V-8 saw the light of day.

The standard six-cylinder AP6 featured the same basic bodywork as its predecessor but had an ornate split grille, different headlights and a new bonnet (which made the car 63 mm longer). Acrylic enamel was introduced and metallic colours were offered for the first time.

Mechanically, there was little change to the standard models, although self-adjusting brakes were now fitted.

August brought the Valiant AP6 V-8, the first 'bent-iron' to be offered by 'The Big Three'. This engine was a 4.4-litre US-built unit taken from the Plymouth Barracuda. It developed 135 kW, produced 352.6 Nm of torque and gave the Valiant a top speed of 175 km/h.

The new V-8 model was available in sedan or wagon body styles, using the same basic bodies as the 'sixes' but distinguished by V-8 emblems and a vinyl-covered steel roof (the Safari wagon came equipped with a roof-rack). The three-speed 'TorqueFlite 8' transmission was standard on both models.

The V-8-engined AP6 was 57 kg heavier than the standard model. To cope with the additional weight and power, the rear suspension was stiffened and a heavy-duty rear axle fitted. Power-assisted brakes were standard.

With this release, the Valiant range comprised ten models (with the Valiant-based Wayfarer utility having been added to the range earlier in the year). The Australian content was now 65 per cent.

43 344 AP6 Valiants were made.□

1966 MINI MOKE

The 'Moke' was a lightweight, multipurpose vehicle produced in Australia by BMC (later Leyland and then JRA Limited) and exported around the world.

Introduced in March 1966, it was for many years Australia's cheapest 'car' and was advertised with the line 'Moking is Not a Wealth Hazard'. Based on Mini Minor components, it was a front-wheel drive vehicle designed for use on and off normal roads. Some 4WD experimental prototypes were built but they never went into production.

The Moke was first built in Britain in the late 1950s. It was intended for use by the armed forces as a light personnel carrier but orders were few. Rather than abandon the project, the parent company transferred production to BMC's Sydney factory.

The Moke had a buckboard-style, all-steel body without doors and windows. This sat on a punt-type chassis structure made from steel pressings. Two seats and a foldaway fabric hood were fitted. Pannier boxes along each side housed the battery, fuel tank and tool kit.

Independent suspension was fitted to all wheels using rubber cones and telescopic shock absorbers, similar to those used on the Morris 850 ('Mini Minor'). The original power plant was a 1-litre BMC Mini engine. In 1977 an updated version, the Californian, was introduced.

When production ceased in March 1981, a total of 26 142 Mokes had been built in Australia. A similar vehicle was produced under licence in Portugal during the mid-1980s.

1966 CHRYSLER VALIANT VC

March 1966 brought the second update of the Valiant AP5 model.

Clever work from Chrysler's styling department made it appear longer and lower, although the overall dimensions were virtually unchanged.

Chrysler advertisements highlighted the new grille and front end treatment and the deep-sectioned bumper bars with their recessed park/turn signal lights. The sedan had a new-look rear with different panels and tail-lights, but the Safari wagon's tail remained virtually unchanged.

The VC used the familiar 'Slant Six' engine, also virtually unchanged. Mechanical refinements included a new steering-column shift, three-speed, all-synchromesh gearbox. A new instrument panel was fitted to all models.

The VC series saw Chrysler attempting a more pronounced model definition, with the three basic variants — Valiant, Regal and V-8 — having individualised exterior ornamentation and different levels of interior trim.

Chrysler offered a high equipment level with the VC. The base model was fitted with windscreen washers, dual-speed electric wipers and fresh-air ventilation. Becoming more safety conscious, Chrysler also fitted full-width instrument panel crash padding, seat belt anchor points, safety door locks and a modified-zone windscreen.

The Regal and V-8 versions had heating and demisting equipment with a two-speed fan booster, full carpeting, central armrests and the three-speed TorqueFlite automatic transmission.

The VC was well received and sales were excellent. By 1967, however, Ford had released the Fairlane 500, which meant that Valiant was no longer the biggest and most powerful of 'The Big Three'. By early 1968 GM-H was also in the act, with the 5-litre Chevrolet V-8 available in its new HK Holden line-up.

65 634 VC Valiants were built.

1966 GM-H HOLDEN HR

Although Holden's HR model, released in April 1966, had only mild styling revisions on the previous HD model, it brought some major mechanical changes.

Enlarged versions of the 'red' motor of 2.65 and 3.05 litres (respectively the '161' and '186') were introduced. There was also a special 109 kW X2 engine available as an option from June 1967.

The HR's new look was subtle but it included many new body panels. A sleeker rear end incorporated new 'tower-type' tail-lights. Wraparound bumpers were fitted and the HR had new front fenders, slim full-length body mouldings, a newly styled roofline and boot lid plus a wider rear windscreen.

There was also a reworked grille with squared-off headlamps and new parking lamps.

The HR was one centimetre lower than the HD, due to low-profile tyres, and the track was widened slightly at the front and rear.

The range of sedans, wagons and light commercials remained the same. The Premier now had a wood-grain finish to its instrument panel and centre console. For the first time, it was offered as a six-seater, with an optional front bench seat.

The HR offered such options as power steering, disc brakes and a limited-slip differential.

In September 1966 six safety items were added as standard equipment. These included windscreen washers, front seat belts and a shatterproof interior rear-vision mirror.

An automatic choke, Holden's first, became available from June 1967.

The HR was a great success, with 252 352 sold.

1966 FORD FALCON XR

The completely new Falcon XR was announced in September 1966 with styling inspired by the incredibly successful US Mustang.

The body shape was not the only thing borrowed; the new Falcon was offered with an optional 4.7-litre '289' V-8 engine taken straight from the Mustang. Equipped with a two-barrel carburettor, this engine produced 150 kW.

The XR was longer, wider and roomier than the previous Falcon XP. The choice of nine models included utility and panel van versions but the two-door hardtops were dropped.

As before, the Falcon sedan and wagon came in three models, although the Deluxe was now called the 500. The option list was further increased with such things as a remote boot release and a stereo tape player.

Ford's big news in April 1967 was the first of the GT Falcons, with a four-speed full synchromesh gearbox and a 168 kW V-8 as standard.

The GT — which was available only in metallic gold — was Australia's fastest production car to date. Boasting a top speed of 194 km/h, it caused enormous excitement among high-performance motorists. The only problem was that the GT was extremely hard to come by because Ford only made enough to comply with the 'Bathurst' homologation regulations.

The Falcon GT was driven to first and second places in the 1967 Gallaher 500 at Bathurst Circuit. In the same year Ford posted 20.5 per cent of passenger car sales and the figure was rising month by month.

XR production amounted to 87 270 units. □

1967 VOLKSWAGEN COUNTRY BUGGY

By February 1967 Volkswagen Australia was losing money. Sales of the locally produced Beetle were disappointing and something new was needed to stem the tide.

With this in mind, VWA designed and built a 'go-anywhere' vehicle to try to break into the lucrative market enjoyed by the Mini Moke and 4WD Land Rover.

The Country Buggy, which was designed at Clayton, Victoria, used VW Beetle and Kombi parts. In some ways it recalled the WW2 German Army Kubelwagen ('bucket car') of the early 1940s.

The prototype Country Buggy — which was heavily promoted by VWA — had foam-filled tanks on each side of the body to make the vehicle amphibious. It also had 317 mm of ground clearance and a power take-off.

In view of this, the bare-as-a-bone production model Country Buggy was a big disappointment. It did not float, was 76 mm closer to the ground and was devoid of a power take-off and most other accessories.

Priced at $1598 (with rear-mounted 1.3-litre engine and four-speed gearbox), it had two seats and a fold-down canvas roof.

Few were sold and production quietly ceased.

1967 FORD FAIRLANE

Ford's remarkable Fairlane has dominated the local luxury market for an unprecedented length of time.

The car had its origins with the US Fairlane which was sold in Australia from the late 1950s. By the early 1960s, the Fairlane was being assembled by Ford Australia and, in March 1967, a locally designed and built Fairlane was released.

Essentially a stretched version of the XR Falcon, the 1967 Fairlane plugged the price gap between the Falcon and the US-built Galaxie.

Offering a higher level of equipment and more room than any other Australian-built car, Fairlane was an immediate success. By 1972 it held 50.3 per cent of the luxury car market.

The Fairlane was available with a choice of two engines — a 3.3-litre, six-cylinder engine and the 4.7-litre Mustang V-8 which developed 150 kW. Two models were offered — the 'Fairlane' and the more upmarket 'Fairlane 500'.

The base Fairlane was priced to compete with the luxury model Holdens and Valiants. At a time when 'big' was 'in', the Fairlane won luxury buyers left, right and centre.

The interior featured wall-to-wall carpet, a walnut finish applique on the dash and an electric clock. Options included automatic transmission, power disc brakes and power steering.

A facelifted version, the Fairlane ZC, was released in July 1969 and a new ZF body was introduced in 1972.

1967 CHRYSLER VALIANT VE

At the end of October 1967, Chrysler released the all-new Valiant VE line-up — the most Australian series to date.

The styling borrowed heavily from the US Dodge Dart and US Valiant, with a long low look and huge expanses of almost flat sheet metal.

With this model, Chrysler achieved its aim of an average of 95 per cent local content.

There were no carryover panels from the VC except the floor plan, which had been considerably altered. The new models had a more aggressive grille treatment, curved side glass, concave rear window and a longer boot line.

The VE was bigger than earlier Valiants with the wheelbase increased by 50 mm to 2740 mm and a wider track. Overall length was up 140 mm.

At the time of the release, there was an 'options war' being waged by GM-H and Ford. Chrysler's response was the high-spec VIP sedan and wagon.

The VIP was lavishly furnished by the standards of the day. It had a V-8 engine, TorqueFlite automatic transmission, coaxial power steering, power-assisted front disc brakes and reclining front bucket seats with built-in adjustable headrests.

There were no less than 18 VE variants. They used the base 'Slant Six' engine of 109 kW, a 120 kW two-barrel carburettor version of the 'Slant Six' and an improved version of the V-8. The V-8 was boosted to deliver 146 kW. Peak torque of 347 Nm was produced at only 2000 rpm.

All VE Valiant models featured dual line brakes, operated by a tandem master cylinder with separate front and rear braking systems (a first for a volume-produced Australian car). Seat belts were fitted to all models.

There were 68 688 VE Valiants made.

1968 GM-H HOLDEN HK BROUGHAM

The all-new Holden HK series replaced the HR in January 1968 and brought Holden's first V-8 engine.

With the HK's bigger, lower, more rounded look, came new names. The base Holden HK was the Belmont and the model formerly called 'Special' became the 'Kingswood'.

The Premier name was retained and a stretched version of the HK, called Brougham, was pitched at Ford's enormously successful Fairlane.

The Brougham sedan, released in July 1968, was over 20 cm longer than the standard sedan despite sharing the same wheelbase and forward panels. The additional length mostly went into the massive boot. This newcomer was equipped with a distinctive grille, a Chevrolet-built '307' V-8 engine, automatic transmission, power steering and the most plush seats yet seen in a Holden.

The HK series offered improved suspension and better sound insulation. The steering was less direct and thus lighter.

GM-H now offered the largest choice of engines, transmissions and interior fittings ever seen in a mass-produced Australian car. The list of options was such that GM-H claimed it was mathematically possible to build two million Holdens and have no two exactly alike.

The 307 Chevrolet V-8 was available for all models including the Belmont.

In July 1968 the HK range was further enlarged with the introduction of the Monaro coupe (see separate entry).

The HK styling was criticised for lack of originality. The Holden sedan was thought to borrow heavily from other makes, especially its main competitor, Falcon.

The HK achieved 199 039 sales. The two-millionth Holden — a Brougham — was produced in 1969.

1968 FORD FALCON XT

The facelifted Falcon XT which replaced the XR model in April 1968 had a few cosmetic changes, a new V-8 engine and an even faster GT.

A 3.1-litre version of the familiar Ford six-cylinder engine was standard, with a 3.6-litre unit optional. The V-8 had a capacity of 4.9 litres and, in standard form, developed 165 kW. Other mechanical improvements included synchromesh on first gear as standard.

The XT Falcon was fitted with a revised grille and distinctive circular tail-lights.

The XT GT version was released shortly after the main range. With the XR series, only a small number of GTs had been made. This time around, the high-performance Falcon was a normal production model.

Power was up to 173 kW and top speed a staggering 200 km/h. And there were some places in Australia where travelling at such a speed was still legal.

Despite all this, the GT failed to win at Bathurst in 1968. It did, however, achieve success in that year's London-Sydney Marathon with 'works' cars finishing third, sixth and eighth and winning the Team Prize. The GT also won the Rothmans 12 Hour Classic at Surfers Paradise.

Never before had it been harder for buyers to choose between a Holden and Falcon. The two cars had reasonably similar styling and were within a centimetre of each other in length and height. GM-H offered four engines for the HK Holden; the XT Falcon had three. Both models had 75-litre fuel tanks, 360 mm wheels, dual circuit brakes and a host of other similarities.

74 394 XT Falcons were built.

1968 GM-H HOLDEN HK MONARO GTS

The Monaro sports coupe, released as part of Holden's HK range in July 1968, was a surprise package designed to boost GM's falling market share.

It was the first Australian vehicle of its type and was expected to bring about the sort of interest that the Mustang had generated in the US.

Based on the HK sedan, the pillarless Monaro shared the same 2800 mm wheelbase and the same overall length.

There were three models using five engines. The base model, simply called Monaro, offered a choice of a 2.65-litre 'six' (the '161'), a 3.05-litre 'six' (the '186') and a 5-litre V-8 (the Chevrolet '307'). The Monaro GTS offered the 3.05-litre '186S' or the Chevrolet '307'. The high-performance Monaro GTS 327 had the same 5.3-litre V-8 engine and four-speed gearbox as the US Chevrolet Corvette.

All V-8 models featured front-wheel disc brakes, a limited-slip differential and rear radius arms for improved axle location.

The GTS 327 version got off to a flying start with victory in the 1968 Hardie-Ferodo 500.

In August 1969 the extremely potent 5.74-litre Chevrolet '350' V-8 was offered with the 'Bathurst Pack' Monaro GTS. This powered Holden's big coupe to its second consecutive Hardie-Ferodo 500 victory.

The Monaro had victories not only in the Hardie-Ferodo 500 but also in the Australian Touring Car Championship and many other motor sport events. By 1971, however, the design had been largely replaced in competition work by the smaller Holden Torana GTR XU1.

The HT and HG versions of the Monaro which followed the HK used the same basic body. In 1971 a redesigned 'HQ' Monaro was released.

1969 HUNTER

The Hunter was a two-door fibreglass-bodied coupe produced in small numbers by Sydney company J & S Fibreglass.

Designed for use on the road and for competition, the Hunter had a tubular chassis, Holden running gear and, usually, a Holden engine.

1969 CHRYSLER VALIANT VF PACER

The surprise of the VF Valiant range — introduced in March 1969 — was a high-performance, four-door sports sedan called Pacer.

The Pacer took Chrysler into unfamiliar teritory. The low-cost model was aimed squarely at the young high-performance motorist.

At the time the VF series was released, Valiant's overall market share was falling marginally. Chrysler's answer was model diversification.

The second new model in the VF range was the luxury Regal 770, marketed to replace the old VIP (which was soon to be replaced by a new bigger VIP).

The VF range also brought a bigger version of the V-8 engine (the 'Fireball 318'), a wider range of seating, more safety features and increased soundproofing. Distinguished from the previous model by a horizontal bar grille, new headlights and new tail-lights, the VF had the front park and turn-indicator lights mounted in the top of the guards.

The Pacer was identified by a black and red grille treatment, red paint-filled boot lid moulding, fake 'mag' wheel covers and narrow, waist-high body striping. It came in three colours — Wild Red, Wild Blue and Wild Yellow — and was powered by a 130 kW high-compression two-barrel version of the 3.69-litre 'Slant Six' engine.

The Pacer had a three-speed floor-shift manual gearbox, finned drum brakes front and rear, a front anti-roll bar and low restriction exhaust system. The suspension was lowered by 12 mm. High-back 'tombstone' seats were fitted.

The Regal 770 — also available only as a sedan — had a high equipment level and was fitted with the new 'Fireball 318' engine developing 172 kW.

In September the VF Valiant Hardtop was announced. The six-model range gave a choice between six-cylinder and V-8 engines and varying levels of equipment. With a 2820 mm wheelbase and a massive tail, the Hardtop's overall length was more than 5000 mm.

There were 52 944 VF Valiants made.

1969 GM-H HOLDEN HT

Holden's HT range, which arrived in May 1969, was only a minor facelift of the HK. But it was the first Australian car to offer a locally designed V-8 engine.

Other features included a 2.5 cm increase in track width, improved suspension and synchromesh on all forward gears.

Minor styling changes were aimed at accentuating the long engine compartment. The model also brought wraparound rear light clusters, a new instrument panel, a new grille and a wider back window.

The locally designed and built V-8 came in two versions. The '253' (4.2 litres) and the '308' (5 litres). The Chevrolet '350' was still available on the Monaro.

The HT model choice still included sedans, wagons, Monaro coupes and the stretched Brougham luxury model. Prices were increased slightly.

An even longer list of options than that offered with the HK gave the new Holden buyer a choice of five engines and four gearboxes, plus the opportunity to add a limited-slip differential, 'Superlift' shock absorbers, disc brakes, power steering, power windows, bucket seats, reclining seats, refrigerated air-conditioning, 'rally' wheels, a vinyl roof and more.

It was in 1969 that the Holden Dealer Team was formed. This team, which was to have countless motor sport victories through the 1970s and 1980s, got off to a brilliant start when Colin Bond drove an 'HDT' Monaro 350 to victory in the 1969 Hardie-Ferodo 500.

183 839 HT sedans and 14 437 Monaro coupes were sold.□

1969 CHRYSLER VIP

In May 1969 the release of the VIP was heralded with the following announcement:

'Chrysler Australia Limited is to enter the luxury segment of larger popular vehicles with a long wheelbase car intermediate between its Valiant range and Dodge Phoenix.

'The new car will be marketed as "VIP By Chrysler".'

Although previous upmarket Valiants had worn the VIP badge, the new version was bigger, dearer and far more luxurious. It was Chrysler's answer to Ford's Fairlane and Holden's Brougham.

The VIP had a wheelbase of 2850 mm — 100 mm longer than the Valiant. Its styling was instantly recognisable as being of the Valiant family but it was distinguished by dual headlights, different rear light treatment, a 'limousine' rear window and a heavily padded vinyl roof.

The engine choice was between the 120 kW 'Slant Six' and the 172 kW 'Fireball 318' 5.2-litre V-8. Automatic transmission was standard with either engine.

Equipment levels were high, with full carpeting, arm-rests on all doors and in the centre of the front and rear seats, heater/demister, dual horns, lights in the engine compartment and boot, courtesy switches and pockets on all doors. Integrated air-conditioning was available as a factory option.

A cheaper version of the VIP was offered with the six-cylinder 120 kW Valiant engine and a front bench seat.

Coaxial power steering and front disc brakes were standard equipment on the V-8 VIP and optional on the 'six'.□

1969 MORRIS 1500 NOMAD

The Nomad, an Australian-engineered reworking of the Morris 1100, was a pioneer hatchback.

The British-designed Morris 1100 had been introduced in Australia in February 1964, replacing the Major Elite. It did well (actually outselling the Mini Minor in 1964) but sales dropped sharply in 1966. BMC responded with a more powerful version of the Morris 1100 called 1500.

The 1500 was launched in June 1969 with a choice between a conventional four-door body style and the five-door Nomad hatchback.

The 1.5-litre, four-cylinder engine developed 55 kW and was coupled to a four-on-the-floor all-synchromesh gearbox. An automatic version was available with a 1.275-litre engine.

In 1970 a five-speed 1500 was released.

Although it recorded reasonable sales, the 1500 did little to reverse the overall sales slump.

BMC's sales continued to fall and its market share, which had been 13 per cent in 1966, was below ten per cent by 1969. This was due largely to Japanese competition and the increasing popularity of larger cars. Morris sold only 17 127 cars in 1970, of which half were 1500 models.

Leyland Australia was formed in 1970 (following the merger of BMC with Leyland in the UK) and the new company started to concentrate on the new Austin XJ six-cylinder model.

1969 FORD FALCON XW

The XW Falcon, released in July 1969, went on to become the biggest selling Falcon so far.

In that year Ford Australia was looking stronger than ever and made it quite clear it intended to be the number one Australian car manufacturer by the mid-1970s.

Essentially a restyled version of the XR/XT series, the XW introduced a 5.7-litre V-8 and the first of the powerhouse GT-HO models.

The long bonnet/short boot look had been a winner, so Ford stuck with it. Minor styling changes included a revised bonnet line and a grille incorporating wraparound traffic indicators and parking lights.

The interior had a new instrument panel, new seat trim combinations and heavier crash-padding.

The XW series reintroduced the Futura name which had disappeared some three years earlier.

The GT now carried gaudy 'Superoo' decals, black bonnet patches, a fake bonnet scoop and quick release bonnet pins. But mechanically it was better than ever. *Wheels* magazine didn't mince words. They simply called it 'Australia's finest production sedan'.

The GT was fitted with the huge US-built 'Windsor 351', a 5.75-litre V-8 producing 225 kW, and had large diameter, ventilated front disc brakes.

In August the 'HO' (Handling Options) package was released. It included a front spoiler, rear stabiliser bar, engine improvements to lift middle-range acceleration and other modifications.

The new XW GT-HO just failed to win at Bathurst in 1969 despite coming first, second and third in the Sandown 3 Hour, the acknowledged Bathurst warm-up.

A new 'Phase Two' Falcon GT-HO with a 5.75-litre 'Cleveland' engine was released in August 1970. With a top speed of 225 km/h, this car provided first and second places at Bathurst in 1970 for works drivers Allan Moffat and Bruce McPhee.□

1969 MORRIS MINI K

Although British-designed, the Morris Mini (or 'Mini Minor') was built in Australia for 18 years and had a major impact on the road and racetrack.

The Mini was originally launched as the Morris 850 in 1959 and went on to record over five million sales. Designed by Greek-born Alec Issigonis, who was also reponsible for the Morris Minor which preceded it, the Mini was the first small car with an engine placed east-west across the front frame, driving the front wheels.

The four-cylinder Mini offered outstanding stability and ease of driving. It became a popular economy car and also fashionable with society people.

The Mini's appeal was further widened by great success in motor sport. By 1970 it had been driven to victory in numerous rallies and races, including the Monte Carlo Rally (three times) and the Gallaher 500 at Bathurst, NSW (in 1966).

The Mini was assembled and partly manufactured in Sydney from March 1961. The first model had an 850 mL engine. Wind-up windows were introduced in 1965 and a 1-litre engine followed in October 1968.

Also produced from 1962 were higher performance versions known as Mini Cooper and Cooper S, with 1-litre and 1.275-litre engines.

Late in 1969 the Mini K was launched. Fitted with a 1.1-litre 38 kW engine and decked with Kangaroo decals, it had an Australian content of 80 per cent.

A new headlight and grille assembly was added in August 1971 and the name became Mini Clubman. Local production continued until September 1978, by which time 176 284 Minis had been built in Australia.

The Mini Minor design proved so successful that by the 1980s almost all small cars had front-wheel drive, east-west engines and incorporated other features pioneered by the Mini.□

1970 CHRYSLER VALIANT VG HARDTOP

For Chrysler, 1970 was 'The Year of the Hemi'.

The Hemi 245 was a completely new US-designed, Australian-developed engine claimed to combine V-8 power with six-cylinder economy.

Chrysler Australia spent around $33 million on the project and called the result 'the most advanced six-cylinder power plant made anywhere in the world'.

Mechanical improvements aside, the VG series continued the same basic sedan, Hardtop and Safari wagon body styles as the previous VF series. To give a fresh look, the new models had rectangular (rather than round) headlights and restyled rear lights.

The Hemi 245 was a 4-litre unit which was lighter and more powerful than the 3.69-litre 'Slant Six' engine it replaced. (The Hemi derived its name from the engine's hemispherical combustion chambers.)

Three versions were offered. A 123 kW Hemi was fitted to the base Valiant and a 138 kW 'two-barrel' (dual-throat carburettor) version with a modified camshaft came with the VIP, Regal 770 sedan and Hardtop. A high-performance two-barrel Hemi was made solely for the Valiant Pacer sports sedan. It developed over 142 kW.

The Hemi received a good reception from the press, which praised its power and even torque qualities.

The 1970 VIP (Chrysler's Valiant-based 'luxury' model) was powered by the 138 kW Hemi 245 with the 172 kW V-8 an option. It was the first Australian-made car fitted with air-conditioning as standard.

In early August, Chrysler combined two popular models and came up with the two-door Pacer Hardtop. It retained most features of the sedan, including the stunning straight-line performance.

Chrysler advertised that the 1970 Valiants had 96 per cent Australian component content. In early 1971 a 3.53-litre '215' Hemi was added to the line-up.

There were 46 374 VG Valiants made. □

1970 GM-H HOLDEN HG

The Holden HG range replaced the HT in July 1970.

It comprised 13 models, with sedans, station wagons, Monaro coupes, a panel van, a utility and the luxurious Brougham model.

There were few differences compared with the previous series, the changes being mostly cosmetic. This was because the HG was released to keep something new in the public eye until the all-new HQ model — GM-H's most ambitious project yet — was ready.

The HG's main mechanical improvement was the introduction of the Australian-built three-speed Tri-Matic automatic transmission. This was standard on the Brougham and available on all other models, except the Monaro GTS 350, which was offered with four-speed manual or the regular two-speed Powerglide automatic.

The HG range featured minor detail changes such as new trim patterns.

The Monaro, now offered with a choice of five engines and four transmissions, had a modified suspension system on the GTS variants. It was designed to give greater comfort.

GM-H sold 155 797 HG models.

1970 GM-H HOLDEN TORANA LC GTR XU1

Torana is an Aboriginal word meaning 'to fly'.

Eventually the 'flying' Holden Torana became famous for its domination on the racetrack — but it had humble beginnings.

The original Torana was the two-door HB model, which was a modified version of the Vauxhall Viva. It was built by GM-H from 1967 with a 1.2-litre, four-cylinder engine. A four-door version arrived in 1968.

The completely new LC Torana — launched in October 1969 with a choice between four-cylinder and six-cylinder engines — was an Australian design.

This new small Holden was much praised and won *Wheels* magazine's 'Car of the Year' award for 1969.

There were eight LC Torana variations, including two and four-door models. The four-cylinder cars still used a Vauxhall engine but the 'sixes' had the '138' — Holden's specially built 2.26-litre Torana unit.

The GTR model was fitted with a two-barrel carburettor '161' (2.64-litre) engine; the high-performance GTR-XU1 model, which became available in August 1970, had a '186' (3.05-litre) engine with three SD Strombergs and other modifications. It developed 120 kW, could hit 194 km/h and cover the standing 400 metres in under 16 seconds.

Fifteen GTR-XU1s were entered for the 1970 Hardie-Ferodo 500; the most successful finished third behind two V-8 Ford Falcons. It was 1972 before a Torana (an LJ model) tasted victory in Bathurst's annual long-distance touring car race. In the interim, the Torana became prominent in all forms of Australian motor sport, winning countless races, rallies, hillclimbs and rallycross events.

GM-H built 74 627 LC Toranas.

1970 BOLWELL NAGARI

The spectacular Nagari sports car was designed and manufactured in Melbourne by Campbell and Graeme Bolwell.

Campbell founded the Bolwell company in 1963; his brother joined three years later after working in Britain under Colin Chapman at Lotus.

The brothers commenced the manufacture of kit cars and, in 1967, they launched the superb-looking Holden-based Mark 7, also sold as a kit but complete with all mechanical parts including a Bolwell-designed suspension system.

One hundred Mark 7s were sold and growing success encouraged the Bolwells to launch their first complete car, called Nagari. It was sold from 1970 and used Ford Falcon components (including a 4.9-litre '302' V-8 engine) with a lightweight fibreglass body and a Lotus-type backbone chassis.

The performance of the Nagari was exceptional. In stock, standard form it could reach 100 km/h in just over seven seconds, cover the standing 400 metres in 14.8 seconds and hit a top speed of 210 km/h.

The majority of Nagaris sold were coupes but a convertible version was also offered.

The Nagari was a big sales success by speciality standards and had some impressive motor sport victories. Rising costs, however, more than doubled the retail price between 1970 and 1974. The brothers had hoped to sell the car in quantity in California, but new emission and safety laws there, as well as in Australia, made the scheme unworkable. By the mid-1970s, the Nagari was dropped and the small Bolwell factory concentrated on industrial fibreglass products. Over 700 Bolwell cars had been produced.

In 1979 Campbell Bolwell announced a new design — the small rear-drive Bolwell Ikara. The prototype had a Volkswagen Golf engine and transmission mounted in the rear, driving the rear wheels. Volume production never started.

1970 AUSTIN X6 KIMBERLY

Following the success of the front-wheel drive Austin 1800 during the late 1960s, British Leyland Australia (formerly BMC, later Leyland Australia) attempted to compete in the Holden/Falcon/Valiant market.

The weapon was the six-cylinder Austin X6.

Powered by a locally designed 2.2-litre east-west mounted engine, the X6 four-door sedan was about 20 cm longer than the 1800. It was the only local family-sized front-wheel drive car on the market and came in two versions, the basic Tasman and the better equipped, more powerful Kimberley. The Kimberley engine had two carburettors and developed 86 kW.

Initial press reactions were favourable but the car soon gained a reputation for poor build quality and reliability.

Despite the company's confident predictions that they would sell 17 500 X6s per year, only 6765 were sold in 1971 and 4367 in 1972.

The considerably improved Mark II versions were launched in 1972 but the damage was done. Leyland's hopes of providing serious competition for 'The Big Three' had failed again.

After the ill-fated P76 model which followed, Leyland Australia withdrew from the manufacturing field. No more Austin cars were sold in Australia but production continued in Britain.□

1970 GM-H HOLDEN TORANA GTR-X

Of all the 'cars that got away', the GTR-X is among the most interesting.

First displayed in August 1970, the sleek two-seater coupe used a fibreglass body and LC Torana running gear.

The body was steel reinforced and included a built-in roll bar. Prototypes were fitted with the 3.05-litre GTR-XU1 '186' engine and extensively tested at GM-H's Lang Lang proving ground.

Promoting the design with lavish brochures, GM-H claimed the GTR-X was designed for low-cost tooling and that limited volume production was being considered.

A mid-1971 release was intended at one stage, with a Melbourne fibreglass company contracted to produce the bodies. Only three prototypes were finished, however, before the whole project was buried. GM-H then changed its story, saying that the GTR-X was only built to gauge public reaction.

It appears that the problems which brought about the end of the project included a shift in public opinion. In the words of one GM-H official: 'In the early 1970s it was becoming socially unacceptable to market "selfish" cars, such as two-seater sports and high-performance models'.

The other problem came from Japan. Nissan had stolen the fire by launching the 240Z coupe in 1970. This was not only selling for less than the projected price of the GTR-X but had an all-steel body. GM-H's marketing men did not think there was room for a second car of that type here.

An earlier Holden sports car — the spectacular V-8 Hurricane — had been built and exhibited in 1969, but this was purely a 'one-off' experimental vehicle.□

1970 FORD FALCON XY

The October 1970 release of the XY Falcon brought new locally designed six-cylinder engines and the most famous performance Falcon of all, the fire-breathing GT-HO 'Phase Three'.

The XY was the final refinement of the XR/XT/XW series and is generally regarded as the best of the breed, having a significantly better performance than the equivalent Holden.

Buyers had a wide choice of standard, Futura and Fairmont models as well as the successful GT and GT-HO performance cars. An even wider range of options than before was offered.

Using the same body as the XW it replaced, the XY was distinguished by a divided plastic grille with wraparound traffic indicators/parking lights. It also had revised tail-lights.

The new model had better seating, more safety features and a quieter, smoother ride.

The new locally designed six-cylinder engines were of 3.3 and 4.1 litres in capacity. The 5-litre and 5.75-litre V-8s were optional in some models and standard in the GTs. A new Selectshift Cruisomatic three-speed automatic transmission was available.

The XY GT was known as 'The Shaker' because of its large centrally mounted bonnet scoop. Unlike the scoop on the XW Falcon GT, this one was functional.

The GT-HO Phase Three model was released in 1971 and could outperform any local production car yet built (see separate entry).

XY production ran to 100 474 units.

1971 CHRYSLER VALIANT VH

With the VH series, released in June 1971, Chrysler at last gave Valiant buyers a uniquely Australian design.

Company executives claimed that four years work and $22 million had gone into the VH.

The new model was wider than the previous model and had an extended wheelbase. It looked enormous, despite the fact that, at 4900 mm, it was only a fraction longer than before.

The VH Valiant's cleaner and more rounded lines were enhanced by a reduction in body decoration. The front parking lights and turning indicator lights were moulded to fit flushly above a curved front bumper bar. A hatch-type bonnet was fitted. A completely new interior complemented the revamped body.

VH buyers were offered two new versions of the much-publicised Hemi engine. These were the '265', a 4.3-litre 'two-barrel' engine producing 152 kW, and a 162 kW version of the same engine fitted to the Pacer sports sedan.

Production of the 4-litre '245' and 3.53-litre '215' continued. The 5.2-litre V-8 was retained as an option on the Regal models.

The medium-line VH Valiant was called the Ranger; the better equipped version became the Valiant Ranger XL. The VH wagon, which was about 152 mm longer than the sedan, featured a massive load space and an integral air-deflector above the rear window.

The prestige Valiant was now the VH Regal. A Regal 770, with a stronger sporting accent, was also available.

The line-up broadened as the year progressed. Chrysler introduced the sensational Charger in August and the 'Chrysler' saloon in November (see separate entries).

The other variant for 1971 was the two-door Valiant VH Hardtop, released in October. Available in Regal and Regal 770 form, it was about 100 mm longer than the VH sedan — and it looked to be all boot. It was a spectacular sales flop; virtually everyone preferred the Charger.

Including Chrysler saloons and Charger models, 67 800 VH Valiants were made.□

1971 GM-H HOLDEN HQ

The completely new HQ Holden was launched in July 1971.

Remarkably, it was the first ground-up redesign of the Holden since it was first sold in 1948.

A massive total of 453 776 HQ sedans was sold, plus 13 782 Monaros. The new Statesman, which came with the HQ series to replace the Brougham, sold 18 092 units.

The six-cylinder engines were carried over from the HG, but with a longer stroke giving 2.84 and 3.3 litres capacity. The new names were the '173' and '202', taken from the cubic inch size.

The HQ was the first Holden fitted with coil spring suspension on all wheels. It also had a subframe.

The HQ series stayed in production for three years — an unusually long period by Holden standards to date. Continuing interest was maintained by a series of 'specials' and variations, such as the 'Vacationer' option package.

In August 1972 a 'four-door Monaro', the sporty SS Holden, was announced. It featured many Monaro details and a 4.2-litre '253' V-8 coupled with a four-speed manual gearbox.

In 1973 a special silver Holden Premier was released to commemorate the 25th anniversary of the Holden car.

The Monaro, now replaced by the Torana XU1 as the prime competition car, continued with a two-door body based on the HQ sedan. The Chevrolet 350 engine was still available, although the car was now being marketed more as a 'grand tourer' than an all-out street racer. In March 1973 a four-door GTS sedan, with virtually the same specs as the Monaro GTS coupe, was released.

Also included in the wide HQ range were utilities and panel vans with full chassis frames. A cab/chassis truck was also added.

The three-millionth Holden was an HQ wagon produced in June 1974.

1971 GM-H STATESMAN

After jealously watching Ford's Fairlane clean up the luxury market, GM-H decided to take positive action by introducing a luxury car bigger than the Holden Premier.

The first Statesman was produced with the HQ Holden range in 1971 as a replacement for the Brougham. It came in two versions — Statesman Custom and Statesman de Ville.

Built on the longer Holden HQ station wagon wheelbase, it was exported to many countries with a different grille and sold as the Chevrolet 350.

Despite a reasonable number of sales, the Statesman never succeeded in matching the phenomenal sales of Ford's Fairlane.

The Caprice version — with a much higher level of equipment — came with the HJ range in November 1974. It featured a 5-litre V-8 engine, automatic transmission and luxurious interior trim.

In 1977 the HZ Statesman, with Holden's acclaimed Radial Tuned Suspension, was released.

The Statesman SL/E followed in 1979. This was fitted with an unusual egg-crate grille and was released largely to use up old-model panels before the release of the redesigned WB Statesman in 1980.

With a fuel crisis and other problems, the SL/E proved so difficult to sell that at one stage dealers made an incredible offer: buyers prepared to pay the full price for a Statesman got a Holden Gemini (the small Isuzu-sourced 'four') thrown in at no extra cost.□

1971 CHRYSLER VALIANT CHARGER VH

The Charger was released two months after the Valiant VH sedans.

It became one of the most remarkable successes in Australian motoring history and, in a scant 12 months, went on to account for almost 50 per cent of all Valiant sales.

The press went wild from the day of release. 'Probably the best-looking car ever produced by an Australian manufacturer' was a typical quote. Not only was the Charger considered good looking, the base Charger was the cheapest Valiant sold.

Although 330 mm shorter and 136 kg lighter than the VH sedan, the Charger was still a five seater. And the smaller dimensions significantly improved handling and performance.

In 1971 sales of two-door cars in Australia were running at 20 per cent of the medium-sized car market. Valiant's new entry generated enthusiasm among a wide selection of buyers.

The Charger used standard Valiant mechanicals and was almost identical to the VH sedan from the windscreen forward. The roofline and rear-end treatment (which included an integral spoiler) were unique.

There were four basic models: Charger, Charger XL, Charger R/T and Charger 770. Each was fitted with a horizontal bar grille with an individualised finish.

The base Charger, powered by the 3.53-litre Hemi 215, was spartan. The Charger XL offered a higher level of equipment and, like the Ranger XL sedan, was the most popular choice of its range.

The most sensational Charger of all was the high-powered R/T (see separate entry), which was pitched at the sporting buyer.

The 770 was the 'luxury' version. It had a plush interior and a unique grey paint treatment of the front grille and rear panel. Vinyl frames decorated the side windows.

Buyers of the 770 had a choice between the 265 high-performance Hemi engine and the 5.2-litre 318 V-8.□

1971 CHRYSLER VALIANT CHARGER VH R/T

A series of immensely powerful R/T Valiant Chargers was developed by Chrysler engineers in 1971 and 1972.

The dual aim was to win the high-performance buyer and take outright honours in the annual Bathurst endurance race.

Distinguished by its grille of red and black bars and quartz halogen driving lights, the R/T had a wide black stripe running from the centre of each door to the rear deck.

A floor-mounted three-speed gearshift was fitted. The regular powerplant was the 162 kW Hemi 265 two-barrel engine, but also available was an 'E37' street version of the Six-Pack Charger engine offered for competition cars.

The E37 used three Italian-made, dual-throated Weber carburettors and developed 186 kW. A full-blown 'E38' racing version of the R/T was also available. It had a 10.5:1 compression version of the 265 engine which produced 210 kW at 5000 rpm and 431 Nm of torque at 3700 rpm.

An additional option was the 'Track Pack', consisting of a 16:1 quick action steering ratio, a 160-litre fuel tank and other accessories. An R/T E38 'Bathurst Special' was released on 5 August 1971.

In June 1972 a four-speed Borg Warner manual transmission was put to work in a new R/T E49 Charger, powered by a Hemi 265 developing a massive 226 kW.

Identified only by a '4' decal on the guard, the 190 km/h-plus E49 could accelerate more quickly than any other production car ever made in Australia. It reached 100 km/h from rest in a shade over six seconds and 160 km/h in just 14.1 seconds.

In late October the Charger 770SE E55 V-8 was released. It had a street version of the four-barrel '340' racing engine but was available only in automatic form.

Unfortunately, none of the high-powered Chargers brought great success in motor sport. The most coveted prize of all — victory at Bathurst — eluded Chrysler and, after 1972, the company decided to concentrate on luxury rather performance.□

1971 NOTA TYPE 4

Nota, a small Sydney-based car manufacturer, has produced a great variety of small-capacity, low-budget sports cars and racing cars.

The road-going Type 4 model, released in 1971, was an open two-seater sports roadster which offered more performance per dollar than just about anything else on the market.

During the late 1950s and 1960s, the Nota firm had produced successful Clubman-type sports cars and front-engined single-seaters which did well in track work. A road-going version of the Clubman-type racer, designed to take Hillman, Fiat, Morris or Coventry Climax engines, was sold in kit form. Nota also built small numbers of open-wheeled racing cars.

In the 1970s a road-going, rear-engined coupe powered by a Leyland P76 V-8 was designed but not completed.

The Type 4 (sometimes known as the 'Fang') was similar in concept to a Clubman but was powered by a Mini Minor engine (usually Cooper S) mounted across the chassis behind the driver.

It had a doorless body of aluminium and fibreglass above a space frame chassis. This lightweight construction gave the Nota excellent acceleration, and features such as four-wheel independent suspension provided first-rate handling.

The Type 4 was extremely basic. Options included a canvas hood.

A total of 105 Type 4s were built before production ceased in 1975. In the mid-1980s the company was still building cars in limited numbers. By this stage their total production had reached about 300 cars.

1971 FORD FALCON XY GT-HO PH. THREE

The GT-HO Phase Three was the world's fastest four-door production sedan.

Built almost exclusively to win the 1971 Bathurst touring car race, the GT-HO Phase Three was instantly recognised as a classic and is now one of the most sought-after Australian cars of all time.

Like the Phase Two, the new GT-HO was a further development of the Falcon GT, with the addition of the Handling Option package to transform it into a thoroughbred race machine.

The Phase Three was more refined than its predecessors and although the maximum speed was not raised, acceleration through the entire speed range was improved. In road-going form, it could top 225 km/h and run the standing 400 metres in a neck-jarring 14.6 seconds.

The GT-HO looked almost identical to the standard XY GT (complete with large 'shaker' bonnet scoop) but had a front and rear spoiler.

Powered by the US-built 'Cleveland' 5.75-litre V-8, the Phase Three had a Holley four-barrel carburettor, reworked head, full extractor system and a string of other performance modifications. Perhaps due to controversy about high-performance road cars, Ford claimed only 225 kW for the Phase Three. In peak tune, it actually delivered 260 kW or more.

The GT-HO scored a devastating 1-2-3 victory in the 1971 Hardie-Ferodo 500. The racing versions were not fitted with a rev-limiter and reached around 240 km/h on Conrod Straight.

Ford built just 200 genuine GT-HO Phase Threes. Three prototype GT-HO Phase Four models, based on the 1972 XA Falcon, were built and tested but only one actually came off the production line before the project was stopped.□

1971 CHRYSLER 'CHRYSLER CH'

The luxurious 'Chrysler by Chrysler' was released in November 1971.

Denoted the 'CH', it was styled on the recently released VH Valiant but built on a longer wheelbase.

With its overall length a fraction under five metres, the Chrysler was designed to take on Ford's Fairlane and GM-H's Statesman, but went one better and offered a two-door Hardtop version as well.

The equipment level was exceptionally high for the day, with power-assisted steering and front disc brakes, tinted power windows, push-button radio with a power-operated antenna, a carpeted boot and a vast variety of interior lights including adjustable reading lights for the rear compartment passengers. The front seat was of an unusual split-bench design.

The Chrysler was distinguished from the Valiant by dual headlights and a bumper bar which encircled the grille.

Two talked-about features were an optional electric-powered seat adjuster and a small light which illuminated the keyhole for 30 seconds after the door had been opened.

The Chrysler was available with a US-designed 5.9-litre V-8, which produced 190 kW. Produced at the Lonsdale plant in South Australia, it was a further development of the Valiant '318' engine, with a larger bore and stroke.

The all-up weight (for the V-8) was a hefty 1077 kg but the top speed was over 175 km/h.

Chrysler's new flagship made a impact, although it never achieved the sales Chrysler had hoped for.

1971 CHRYSLER VALIANT GALANT

Australia's 'little Valiant' came about after the US Chrysler Corporation bought a large shareholding in the Japanese Mitsubishi company.

Mitsubishi was on the rise, having found international acceptance in the 1960s with the Colt design.

The first Colt had appeared in 1962 and was sold in Australia from 1964. In August 1971 Chrysler Australia announced an agreement whereby it would assemble Colt Galants and sell them as Chryslers.

The first 'Valiant' Galant, the GA model, was a small front-engined, rear-drive sedan available in 1.3-litre and 1.5-litre versions. In 1972 the GB model introduced 1.4-litre and 1.6-litre engines and in 1973 a five-door wagon was offered. In 1974 the facelifted GC version appeared.

A fully imported GC 'Hardtop' two-door was added to the line-up.

By the time the GD series was released in 1976, 52 000 Valiant Galants had been sold. Local content was 60 per cent.□

1972 GM-H HOLDEN TORANA LJ

In 1972 a Torana won the prestigious Hardie-Ferodo 500 at the Bathurst Circuit.

In that year, the XU1 Toranas also took the lion's share of major rallies and rallycross events and won most series production car races.

Following this phenomenal motor sport success, it is easy to overlook that the 'little Holden' was also an extremely successful family car.

The LJ replaced the LC in March 1972. It had a new HQ Holden-style grille, wraparound tail-lights, a revised instrument panel and new bucket seats.

The engine choice comprised 1.2-litre, 1.3-litre and 1.6-litre, four-cylinder units and three six-cylinder engines. The GTR-XU1 model had a 143 kW, 3.3-litre 'six', giving a top speed of over 200 km/h and dazzling acceleration. In the spirit of the age, it was available in a range of garishly bright colours.

During 1972, the Holden Dealer Team (GM-H's unofficial motor sport arm) built a 5.05-litre V-8-engined Torana. This was a prototype vehicle for a V-8 XU1 (sometimes referred to as the XU2) intended for the Hardie-Ferodo 500 in October.

An outcry against 'supercars' forced GM-H to withdraw from the project but the highly developed 'six' (and the mastery of driver Peter Brock) was enough to give Torana victory at Bathurst in 1972. But for a pit-crew miscalculation on fuel consumption, Brock's Torana could have won again in 1973.

A total of 81 453 LJ Toranas was built.

1972 Gvang

1973 Leyland P76

1975 Ilinga AF2

1977 Purvis Eureka

1977 Holden Torana LX A9X Hatchback (courtesy Modern Motor magazine)

1982 Holden Camira JB

1985 Triad

1986 Falcon XF

1986 Mitsubishi Magna Elite

1986 Nissan Pintara

1986 Holden Commodore VL Calais

1972 FORD FALCON XA

The XA model was the first Falcon completely designed and manufactured in Australia.

Released in March 1972, it had an entirely new body and, for the first time in seven years, a two-door hardtop version was included in the range.

'More of everything' was the theme to this Falcon line-up. The XA had more power than the XY model it replaced and a wider choice of engines, a longer list of options and a bigger, more roomy body. For the first time, Falcon had a full flowthrough ventilation system.

Ford claimed to have put four years work into the new model. When it was released, Ford was less than one percentage point behind GM-H in total market share and an even fiercer battle was in the making.

The XA came in Falcon, Falcon 500, Futura, Fairmont and Falcon GT versions. A choice of six engines included two locally produced V-8s (4.9-litre and 5.75-litre) and a wide range of transmissions was offered.

The XA Hardtop was introduced in August. Ford was at last ready to mount a strong challenge to the Valiant Charger and Holden Monaro coupes.

Ford officials claimed the Hardtop — which came in three models — was the best looking car ever produced in Australia. Based on the XA sedan, it was roughly the same length as the sedan but lower and wider. It used similar mechanical components and was marketed as the 'Supreme Falcon'.

A 255 kW GT-HO 'Phase Four' based on the XA model was planned for release in time for the 1972 Bathurst race, but it was shelved following political and media objections to 'super cars'.

The XA Hardtop was used in competition from August 1973. It was an immediate success and was driven to victory in the extended 1000 kilometre Hardie-Ferodo of 1973.

The XA series continued in production until late 1973, by which time 129 473 units had been built.

1972 GVANG

The Gvang — a futuristic high-performance steam car — is one of many promising Australian designs which have never made it to the showroom floor.

Built in Sydney in the early 1970s, the Gvang was fitted with a highly unorthodox two-cylinder steam engine which developed 300 kW.

The engine, which was mounted between the rear wheels, had a nominal capacity of 2.9 litres. It featured oscillating pistons and an electronically controlled generator which automatically monitored and controlled the steam supply. Because of the enormous amount of torque produced at low engine speeds, no clutch or gearbox was necessary.

The name Gvang was derived from the name of the designer, Gene van Grecken, an artist and architect. He designed the entire vehicle with some help from Bob Britton and Stan Smith. The prototype, with a locally-made stressed aluminium body, was exhibited at Sydney's 1972 International Motor Show.

According to van Grecken, the Gvang had a theoretical top speed of 320 km/h. He intended to publicly demonstrate the design by beating the land speed record for steam-powered vehicles. The project eventually ran out of funds and did not proceed past the prototype stage. □

1972 FORD CORTINA TC 'SIX'

With a locally built six-cylinder engine shoehorned into the front, the unexciting Cortina became a excellent performer.

The medium-sized Cortina family car had first appeared on the Australian market in September 1962. It was an English-made two-door sedan with a 1.2-litre, four-cylinder engine.

The local Ford company re-engineered a later Cortina design and made a car that was unique to Australia. Launched as the Cortina TC in September 1972, it was fitted with the Falcon 3.3-litre 'six' engine. An optional 4.1-litre 'six' was also available. A large bulge in the bonnet was necessary to make room for the bigger engine. An updated TD six-cylinder Cortina was produced from October 1974.

From July 1977 the completely new-look Cortina TE was available, also with a six-cylinder engine. The design was based on the German Taunus but incorporated substantial modifications for Australian road conditions as well as changes to accommodate the Falcon engine. The alternative four-cylinder engine was British and the transmission was made in New Zealand.

The TE remained on sale until 1980 when the revised TF was launched. Production in Australia was discontinued in 1981.□

1972 FORD FAIRLANE ZF

By 1972 Ford no longer had the big car market to itself.

The top-selling Fairlane faced spirited competition from GM-H's Statesman and the Chrysler saloon.

Ford responded with the ZF Fairlane, based on the all-Australian XA Falcon. The ZF maintained the same wheelbase as the previous Fairlane but was lower and wider.

It featured increased interior room and was smoother, quieter and more plush than its predecessor. A distinctive grille had eight horizontal bars and twin side-by-side headlamps.

The new model was sold in two versions — the Fairlane Custom and the more upmarket Fairlane 500. Engine choice was between a 4.1-litre 'six', and 4.9-litre and 5.75-litre V-8 engines.

A facelifted version, the ZG, was released in November 1973 with a four-horizontal-bar grille. The body was identical to the ZF.

The major criticism of the ZF/ZG series was that it looked too much like the smaller, cheaper Falcon. Ford rectified this in 1976 with the bigger ZH model.

1973 CHRYSLER VALIANT VJ

Although released at a time when Chrysler's market share was falling, the Valiant VJ sold 90 865 units, making it the biggest-selling single Valiant model.

The heydays of the 60s were gone (the VJ took nearly three years to achieve its sales) but Chrysler had a new quality-conscious approach and was determined to fight back.

The VJ was a refinement of the 1971 VH. It brought no new sheet metal, styling changes being restricted to the grille, new round headlights and revamped tail-lights.

With sales still suffering as a result of quality-control problems with the VH, Chrysler elected not to build a 'new' Valiant but to market a better equipped and better built version of the existing design.

The VJ's major mechanical improvement was an electronic ignition system fitted to the more expensive models. This was a 'first' for an Australian-built car. Among the small number of other changes, new seats were added across the range, a different steering wheel was fitted and Chrysler introduced the first local metric speedometer.

After the expensive exercise of offering 56 variations in the VH range, Chrysler rationalised its line-up. Only 18 VJ models were offered (the R/T Charger being the most notable casualty), but the option list was lengthened.

The Charger had easily been Australia's top-selling two-door during the previous year but, strangely, the accent was now on luxury rather than the low-price/high-performance formula which had made it such a success. The VJ Charger's grille treatment had a pillar effect and round headlights.

The Chrysler 'CJ' limousine went on sale in early April of 1973, with small changes to styling and body decorations.

Chrysler finished 1973 with a dismal 9.5 per cent market share. For the first time it was behind a Japanese company (Toyota).

In July 1974 Chrysler announced a large rise in the equipment levels. But it had become obvious that stronger action was needed if the sales decline was to be arrested. □

1973 LEYLAND P76

Often thought of as 'Australia's Edsel', the boldly conceived P76 was a monumental failure.

It was launched to boost the ailing Leyland Motor Corporation of Australia (formerly BMC Australia and British Leyland Motor Corporation of Australia Ltd) but instead hastened the demise of the company's local manufacturing operations.

The P76 (named after its original drawing board number) was a completely new sedan designed as a 'European flavoured' competitor for Holden, Falcon and Valiant.

Styled by Michelotti in Italy and designed by Leyland engineers in Sydney, the P76 was conventionally engineered. The standard model had a six-cylinder engine of 2.6 litres but an optional 4.4-litre V-8 was available. Based on the Rover 3.5 unit, the locally made V-8 developed 144 kW, making the P76 one of the most powerful family cars of its day.

The car's unusual wedge-shaped body incorporated a luggage compartment so large it could take a 200 litre oil drum. The P76 had an overall length of 4.88 metres and a weight exceeding 1200 kg. Rack-and-pinion steering and front-wheel disc brakes were fitted.

Launched in June 1973, after dozens of false starts and hiccups, the P76 quickly gained a reputation for poor quality control. Furthermore it was launched at a time when smaller cars were becoming fashionable.

By late 1974 Leyland found itself in desperate financial trouble and was forced to withdraw from local manufacturing. The company sold its vast Zetland plant to the Australian Government but carried on some car assembly work (mainly Minis, Mokes and Land Rovers) at Enfield.

A coupe version of the P76, called Force 7, was ready for production when Leyland's local manufacturing operations collapsed (see '1974 Leyland Force 7' entry). A P76 station wagon, designed earlier, had been shelved. □

1973 FORD LANDAU

Not content with outselling all other locally made luxury cars with the Fairlane, Ford went further upmarket in August 1973 to 'take on the Europeans'.

Their weapon was the most expensive car produced in Australia to that time, available in four-door form, as the LTD and in two-door form as the Landau.

Ford Australia had been selling the gigantic American Galaxie LTD limousine since 1970 but the 1973 LTD was the first locally made car bigger than the Fairlane.

The Landau was described as a two-door 'personal coupe'. Like the LTD and Fairlane, it used XB Falcon mechanical components.

The standard equipment list included integrated air-conditioning, '351' V-8 engine, automatic transmission, electric windows and push-button radio. These models were the first Australian-built cars equipped with disc brakes on all wheels.

Both cars had the same front-end styling; the Landau (based on the Falcon coupe) had a 2820 mm wheelbase, the LTD had a 3085 mm wheelbase and cost an extra $800.

The LTD was 130 mm longer than the Fairlane but its side-on profile was very similar.

In 1975 Ford built a limited edition gold-coloured LTD, known as the Cartier LTD, to commemorate its 50 years in Australia.

In 1976 the Landau was dropped but a facelifted LTD was released. It featured a distinctive new radiator plus reworked front and rear bodywork. A special 'Silver Monarch' version was offered with silver paint, silver vinyl roof and dark red interior trim.

By 1979 the LTD used the same wheelbase and body panels as the Fairlane.

1973 FORD FALCON XB HARDTOP

The facelifted Falcon XB was released in September 1973 after a troubled time for Ford.

With the impressive 1972 XA model, Ford had been widely tipped to catch and pass GM-H in the sales race. But various problems, including a nine-week-long strike, led to Ford suffering a drop in its market share.

What's more, the medium size car market was shrinking due to rises in the price of fuel.

Despite this, the XB was a great success and went on to become the biggest-selling Falcon to that date. In 1970 Ford officials had announced a ten-year plan to overtake Holden as Australia's most popular car. In December 1973 Ford outsold GM-H for the first time in any one month.

Fitted with a distinctive honeycomb grille, the XB had 'cleaner' front and rear styling treatments. Features included front-wheel disc brakes (as standard), a multifunction steering-column stalk, a full synchromesh manual gearbox, inertia reel seat belts and a new type of safety steering column. The wagon was available with an extra bench seat in the rear compartment.

Ford Australia had withdrawn its support from motor racing by the time the XB was released but many drivers continued to race Falcons. Allan Moffat had a car specially prepared in the US for the 1974 Hardie-Ferodo 1000. He failed to finish but another Falcon, driven by John Goss and Kevin Bartlett, scored a brilliant wet track victory. Not one of the three Falcons entered in the 1975 race, however, made it to the finish.

The XB had an unusually long run of nearly three years, during which 211 971 were sold, a production record for Ford Australia.

1974 GM-H HOLDEN TORANA LH

The Torana was originally released as the 'little Holden'. By the time the LH model arrived in March 1974, the picture had changed drastically.

The LH had a significantly larger body than the LJ model it replaced and it was actually bigger than the early model full-sized Holdens.

The new Torana was available only as a four-door sedan. It offered a range of six-cylinder engines and, for the first time, an optional V-8.

In March 1974 the four-cylinder Torana TA was also unveiled, being virtually an LJ Torana (still in two-door or four-door versions) with a new grille and wraparound tail-lights.

GM-H was determined to keep building on the Torana's remarkable motor sport record. The high-performance version of the LH was the 5-litre V-8 SL/R 5000. It was further improved later in the year by the L34 options pack which lifted power and raised the top speed to around 250 km/h.

Torana was driven to victory in the 1974 Australian Touring Car Championship (by Peter Brock, who used his six-cylinder GTR-XU1 for the first three races, then the V-8 SL/R 5000 for the last two) but came second to a Falcon in that year's Hardie-Ferodo 1000.

In 1975 Toranas took the first four places in the Hardie-Ferodo (and won the Australian Touring Car Championship); in 1976 they took the first seven places in the Hardie-Ferodo.

Meanwhile, as a road car, Torana was outselling its Ford and Chrysler rivals (the Cortina and Centura) combined.□

1974 GM-H HOLDEN HJ

The facelifted Holden HJ replaced the HQ in October 1974.

During a run of over three years, the HQ had sold extremely well. Nearly 500 000 were built but towards the end of the production run Ford was seriously threatening GM-H's leadership.

For some months of 1974 Ford outsold GM-H in the full-sized family car market section.

The HJ was distinguished by differently styled grilles, wraparound front and rear lights, larger bumpers and slight revisions of the front-end sheet metal.

Interior changes were also minor. There were full-foam seats, a new dashboard, a revised ventilation system and other upgraded equipment.

The Kingswood, by far the biggest-selling model, now came with the 3.3-litre engine and power-assisted disc brakes.

Dropped from the range was the 350 Chevrolet-engined Monaro. At the beginning of November, the 'HJ' Statesman (GM-H's extended luxury model) was announced. The range included a new 'Caprice' version of the Statesman, which was the most luxurious car GM-H had produced.

GM-H built 154 114 HJ sedans, 4754 Monaros and 8383 Statesmans.

1974 LEYLAND FORCE 7

Leyland's Force 7 nearly became the first locally designed hatchback on the Australian market.

But by the time the first models were coming off the production line, Leyland Australia was in terrible financial trouble.

Many people believed the new two-door Leyland had the potential for success but the company closed its Australian manufacturing operations before a single Force 7 was sold.

The Force 7 was based on the Leyland P76 and shared the same wheelbase, floor plan and mechanical components. The overall length however, was chopped by 23 cm without reducing the interior room. The rear seat folded to reveal an area big enough for two adults to sleep.

Initially the Force 7 was to be sold only with the P76 4.4-litre alloy V-8, but the P76's 'six' would probably have been available later as an option.

An upmarket 'Tour de Force' version was to be offered with air-conditioning, stereo sound, power steering and automatic transmission.

Though the styling of the Force 7 was in some ways similar to the P76, they shared no common body panels.

When Leyland was forced to shut down its manufacturing operations late in 1974, many partially built Force 7s were destroyed. Nine complete cars survived and were auctioned.

After 1974, Leyland Australia concentrated on importing a range of luxury cars, mainly Jaguar, Rover and Triumph and later Range Rover. In March 1983 Leyland Australia changed its name to JRA Limited. By 1986 JRA was one of Australia's most financially successful car companies.

1975 ILINGA AF2

Few local car projects have been more ambitious than the high-class Ilinga AF2.

Dubbed 'Australia's Ferrari', the Ilinga was extremely well received but the project collapsed after only two cars were made.

Ilinga Pty Ltd spent $200 000 developing the AF2 prototype. The car was announced in February 1975 with a plan to manufacture 100 units a year. The proposed retail price was $16 000.

The four-seater coupe was powered by a Leyland 4.4-litre, P76 V-8 engine developing 165 kW and giving a 200 km/h top speed. The body was based on a 'safety cell' structure, sitting on a box section chassis. The design ensured that in the event of a collision, the engine would be pushed under the passenger compartment.

The Ilinga's equipment list was most impressive. It included automatic transmission, air-conditioning, foam-filled petrol tanks, aluminium alloy body panels, Recaro seats, ventilated disc brakes, stereo sound and remote-control door locking. A novel feature was a folding umbrella which fitted into a compartment within the driver's door.

Ilinga Pty Ltd announced it would produce a maximum of 300 of the original design, then replace it with a more advanced model in 1978. As it turned out, the company built only two cars before winding down the project. The reasons were never made clear but they probably centred around supply difficulties with the engines, transmission and body panels.

1975 CHRYSLER CENTURA KB

The Centura was a cosmopolitan car assembled in Australia using imported Simca and locally made Valiant mechanical components.

Originally designed in Britain and built in France as the Chrysler 180, the car was given a new look and power train for Australia. The first Centura parts arrived here in 1973 but industrial action prevented their being assembled. The car was not officially released until March 1975.

The conventionally designed four-door sedan was offered with three engines: an imported 2-litre, four-cylinder unit (90 kW), the Valiant Hemi 3.5-litre 'six' (105 kW) and the Valiant 4-litre 'six' (124 kW).

In June 1977 the KC model replaced the original KB and the four-cylinder variant, which had been outsold by the 'six' at a ratio of three-to-one, was dropped.

Production ceased around the end of 1977 but Chrysler still had sufficient stock to sell through most of 1978.

1975 PRITCHARD

The Pritchard was an unusual vehicle powered by a radical steam engine.

The first Pritchard was produced in Melbourne in 1963 and about six different vehicles were built over the next 20 years. The originator of the design, Arnold Pritchard, died in 1968 but his son Ted carried on the work until the mid-1980s.

The Pritchards developed a vee-type of poppet valve engine with a flash boiler of their own design. They claimed it to be far superior to conventional petrol-powered or steam-powered units and attracted many financial backers. Over $1 million was spent on development, including funds provided by the Federal and Queensland Governments.

There were some promising signs, including an option taken by a major US company, but the design never went into production.

Ted Pritchard once claimed that the car would start in 45 seconds, cruise at 136 km/h and use only 9.4 litres of fuel per 100 kilometres. The engine could run on a variety of fuels, including alcohol and solid fuels.

The Pritchard was one of two ambitious post-WW2 attempts to launch an Australian steam car. The other was the 1972 Gvang.

1975 CHRYSLER VALIANT VK

By the time the VK Valiant was released, Chrysler — once considered a design leader — was clearly years behind its major rivals.

The VK, like the VJ before it, was based on the 1971 VH model.

Chrysler directors called it a 'stopgap' and said an all-new model would be released shortly. Meanwhile they tried to sell a big car in a fuel crisis atmosphere, to a market which was more environmentally conscious than ever before.

The VK had a new grille treatment and revamped tail-light assembly plus a few changes to the ornamentation and nameplates. Some small interior changes were also made.

Further rationalisation of models and options took the model choice down from 11 to eight: Chrysler sedan, Regal sedan and wagon, Ranger sedan and wagon, Charger XL and 770 and Dodge utility. The option list was also trimmed.

The Valiant, Valiant Regal and Valiant Charger were now known as Chrysler Valiant, Chrysler Regal and Chrysler Charger.

All models with six-cylinder Hemi engines were equipped with a new 'clean' Carter carburettor. The 'Fuel Pacer' — a vacuum device using a flashing light to help the driver avoid fuel wastage — was offered as an option.

New safety features included a pressure-sensitive proportioning valve (to reduce the possibility of rear-wheel lock-up during braking), power-boosted brakes and hazard warning lights.

Another feature was a steering-column control stalk for the turn signals, windscreen wipers, washers and high-beam. This was the first multipurpose stalk control from 'The Big Three'.

Five Chrysler engines were offered. The '360' (5.9-litre) was available as an option on most models, including the Ranger sedan and Charger 770.

20 555 VKs were made — the smallest Valiant production run since the S Series.□

1976 FORD FAIRLANE ZH

The new, bigger 1976 Fairlane hit the showrooms at a time when Ford's luxury car sales were lower than they had been for years.

The previous ZF/ZG series had been criticised for looking too much like the Falcon — and so the Ford designers pulled out all stops to make the ZH model distinctive.

Fairlane's problems had not only been caused by its looks. GM-H was offering strengthened competition with its Statesman and Caprice and the sales of European cars were increasing dramatically.

Volvo was now capturing 22.7 per cent of the luxury market and Fairlane's share had dropped from a 1972 high of 50.3 to just over 27 per cent in 1975.

Ford claimed the ZH Fairlane represented four years development work. It was launched in May 1976 in '500' and 'Marquis' models, with a choice of 4.9-litre and 5.75-litre V-8 engines. Automatic transmission was standard equipment.

Not only was the ZH distinctive in appearance, it was unusually large. In fact, the Fairlane was now 18.7 mm longer than its former 'big brother', the LTD.

One marketing device used by Ford for the ZH was a more extensive options list.

In May 1978 the Fairlane 500 and Marquis were upgraded with additional equipment and some carburettor changes to improve the fuel consumption.

1976 GM-H HOLDEN HX MONARO 'LE'

GM-H updated the Holden HJ (in turn an updated HQ) with the HX and released it in July 1976.

The major change was a low-emission version of each Holden engine.

These modified engines were fitted to ensure all Holdens met the stringent new anti-pollution standards demanded by Australian Design Rule 27A. As a result, engine power dropped sharply.

The HX had a new grille, revised hubcaps and other minor modifications. The biggest improvement from a driver's viewpoint was a steering-column stalk (in all models) giving fingertip control of the wipers, washers, turn signals, headlight dipper and flasher.

Towards the middle of 1976, GM-H stopped building Monaro coupes. In September the company cleared its factory of Monaro panels by assembling 600 'LE' (Limited Edition) luxury Monaro coupes.

Equipped with just about every option known to GM-H, the 5-litre V-8 LE had air-conditioning, quadraphonic cartridge tape player, power windows, automatic transmission, front and rear spoilers, metallic paint with gold pin striping, honeycomb polycast wheels and more.

Later in 1976 a special silver HX sedan marked 50 years of General Motors in Australia.

110 669 HX Holdens were produced.

1976 FORD FALCON XC

The XC Falcon was a facelifted version of the big-selling XB and, sadly, it spelled the end of the line for the legendary Falcon GT.

Released in July 1976, the XC featured cosmetic changes and a lowered beltline to give better visibility and a more modern profile.

The main changes were mechanical. The engine had to comply with newly introduced exhaust emission regulations, so the six-cylinder unit featured a reworked cross-flow cylinder head. The same 3.3-litre and 4.1-litre cylinder blocks were retained.

By using the new cylinder head, Ford met the incoming laws with minimal problems (actually increasing the performance for some engines) while GM-H's Holden suffered a severe power drop. Furthermore, Ford was getting good mileage from publicising its superior suspension and handling.

Many Falcon features previously listed as options were standard equipment on the XC. The new model had a revised interior and instrument panel layout.

As well as phasing out the GT, Ford stopped producing the low-volume Futura. Eight months after the announcement of the new model, the Falcon range was expanded to include XC Hardtop variants.

Ford was going better than ever, but Holden hit back hard with 'RTS' — an improved suspension/handling package. In May 1978 Ford answered with a modified suspension for the whole range, greatly improving the handling and ride.

This 'XC½', as it became known, also included some trim changes and is distinguished by an oval Ford badge in the centre of the grille.

The limited edition Cobra two-door hardtop, introduced in August 1978, was the last of the two-door Falcons (see separate entry).

171 082 XC Falcons were built.

1976 CHRYSLER VALIANT CL

The Valiant CL, released October 1976, was a disappointment for those awaiting the promised all-new model.

Major styling changes (including new sheet metal for the first time in three models) gave the Valiant a substantially new look front and rear but again the car was essentially a remodelled VH.

The choice of models, engines and options was again reduced. The prestige CL was now the Regal SE, fitted with the 5.2-litre V-8. Built on the regular Valiant's 2810 mm wheelbase, it replaced the long wheelbase Chrysler saloon.

To meet the ADR 27A anti-pollution legislation, the base Valiant sedan and wagon had a low-compresssion 4-litre, six-cylinder Hemi 245 engine.

The Charger coupe, which commanded ever-decreasing sales, was now available in just one model — the 770 — fitted with a honeycomb grille.

In April 1977 Chrysler Australia announced its first Valiant panel van. Based on the utility, it was offered with two option packages, the 'Sports Pack' and 'Drifter Pack', designed to give youth appeal. The Drifter Pack included bold exterior paint and decals plus the 4.3-litre Hemi 265 engine and four-speed manual transmission.

For the year of 1977, Chrysler Australia reported a loss of $28 million.

In April 1978 Chrysler responded to GM-H's 'Radial Tuned Suspension' with a new suspension package to improve the CL's handling, roadholding and steering.

At the same time, the 5.2-litre '318' V-8 was fitted with the 'Electronic Lean Burn System' (ELB). This engine management system comprised an analog spark control computer and a more efficient carburettor.

The suspension changes and ELB were put to work in the Chrysler 'Le Baron', an upmarket CL, with metallic silver paint and a silver vinyl roof.

A total of 32 672 CL models was made, including the 500 000th Australian Valiant.

1977 GM-H HOLDEN TORANA LX A9X

The LX Torana range, released in October 1976, introduced the first locally made hatchback body style and later brought the most potent Torana of all, the A9X.

The LX hatchback was available with a 3.3-litre, six-cylinder engine, 4.2-litre V-8 or 5-litre V-8 (on the 'SS' variant). There were also three sedan variants.

Finding that the big-engined Toranas were overshadowing the four-cylinder model, the GM-H marketing men gave the 'four' a new lease of life as the 'Sunbird'. This was fitted with a 1.9-litre engine and was the first Holden to feature the 'Radial Tuned Suspension' handling package.

In August 1977 the A9X performance pack was quietly released to enable GM-H to homologate parts required for racing. Only 500 Toranas were fitted with this option, including hatchback and sedan versions.

The A9X pack gave the 5-litre V-8 Torana four-wheel disc brakes (a first for Holden), 14 inch (36 cm) wheels, wheel arch flares, upgraded suspension, Salisbury rear axle, electric engine fan, bonnet air-scoop and other equipment.

An extremely tall differential ratio was fitted to increase the top speed on Bathurst's Conrod Straight. In the 1977 race, the specially prepared A9Xs topped 260 km/h.

Despite this tall gearing, the 161 kW/400 Nm road-going Torana could sprint to 100 km/h in under eight seconds and cover the standing 400 metres in about 15.8 seconds. 100 km/h could be reached without moving out of first gear.

Although the A9X Torana failed at Bathurst in 1977, it soon completely dominated production car racing. In 1978, A9Xs finished first and second in the Hardie-Ferodo 1000; in 1979 they took the first eight places.

Shortly after its release, the A9X was described by *Wheels* magazine as a vehicle which 'deserves to take its place at the very top of the supercar pile along with the Phase Three GT-HO'. When production stopped, good second-hand examples were soon changing hands for much more than the original new price.

41 375 LX sedans and 8527 LX hatchbacks were produced.

1977 DATSUN 200B

The Datsun 200B was Nissan Australia's first attempt to produce a uniquely Australian vehicle.

Designed as a replacement for the 180B, it was announced in October 1977 and was sold with a choice of sedan or wagon body styles.

Larger, heavier and more powerful than the 180B, the 200B was different to its Japanese equivalent. It had a larger engine, a different suspension set-up and a much higher level of equipment.

The 200B was powered by a front-mounted, 2-litre, four-cylinder engine driving the rear wheels.

At first only the sedan version was manufactured in Australia, with a 200B wagon being built in Japan to the Australian specifications. By 1978, however, a locally built wagon was on sale.

A 200B hardtop coupe, the 'SSS', was imported in 1977.

In June 1978, mainly to counter the Sigma, Nissan introduced the sportier 200B SX. Numerous changes were also made to the standard 200B over the following years and a much-improved product resulted.

The 200B remained in production until mid-1981 when it was replaced by a more modern-looking car which reverted to the original name of Bluebird.

Interestingly, although the Datsun 200B was Nissan Australia's first uniquely Aussie model, Datsuns had been sold in Australia over 40 years earlier.

The first Nissan assault on the Australian market was a shipment of 24 Datsun Phaetons landed in 1934. Based on the British Austin 7, the Phaeton was an amalgam of British and Japanese parts. □

1977 GM-H HOLDEN HZ SANDMAN VAN

The Holden HZ, released in October 1977, was another revision of the HQ model, which had made its appearance six years before.

By this time, GM-H had built 3.6 million Holdens — a far greater number anyone had thought possible in 1948.

The HZ was the first full-sized Holden with GM-H's Radial Tuned Suspension, which had already been fitted to the smaller Holden Sunbird and Torana.

The aggressive marketing of RTS led to a so-called 'handling war' between 'The Big Three', with Ford and Chrysler both releasing their own revised suspension systems.

Other Holden changes were minor and included upgraded interior trim.

The range consisted of wagon and sedan versions of Kingswood SL and Premier, a GTS sports sedan and light commercials including the Sandman van and utility. The Belmont sedan was dropped; the Monaro having been discontinued towards the end of 1976.

New Statesman variants were announced shortly after the Holden HZ range was announced.

The Sandman panel van and utility had been released with the HX range to cater for the fastest-expanding section of the market — the recreational field. They were continued with the HZ range, with 'GTS' exterior treatment and trim and a 4.2-litre V-8 as standard.

The HZ stayed in production until 1980 and was the last of the traditional-sized Holdens. At first, the range was supplemented — and then replaced — by the smaller and lighter Commodore based on a German Opel design.

154 155 HZ Holdens were sold.

1977 PURVIS EUREKA

The Purvis Eureka has become the most successful Australian specialist sports car ever produced.

The Eureka was first seen in 1974 when ex-advertising executive Allan Purvis exhibited the original model at the 1974 Melbourne Auto Show. This model — based on the 1971 British-made Nova — was later extensively restyled.

The Eureka was built in Dandenong, Victoria, and consisted of a fibreglass coupe body mounted on a standard Volkswagen Beetle chassis platform. Sold both as a complete vehicle and as a kit car, it used existing VW mechanical components, new or second-hand.

On the original version the turret canopy was raised or lowered by hand to fully enclose the occupants. Later a power mechanism was offered as an option.

The Eureka features an unusually low height and weight, ensuring its performance is much brisker than that of a standard VW.

By 1986 over 500 Eurekas had been sold. The 1986 Purvis Eureka is powered by a 1.6-litre VW aircooled engine and is claimed to have a maximum speed of 180 km/h.

A spectacular mid-engined convertible is scheduled for production in the late 1980s. Called the Free Spirit, it will probably use Ford Laser running gear.

1978 GM-H HOLDEN SUNBIRD UC

The UC range, announced in March 1978, brought four Sunbird and three Torana models, with sedan and hatchback body styles.

They had square headlights, extensive new front-end styling to give a more rounded appearance and substantial mechanical improvements, including Radial Tuned Suspension (RTS).

When introduced with the Torana LX range in late 1976, the Sunbird had been the first Holden equipped with the new RTS, a feature later extended to all Holden cars.

The Sunbird UC (like the LX) was essentially a Torana fitted with a German-made 1.9-litre, Opel four-cylinder engine. Buyers were offered a four-speed manual or three-speed automatic transmission.

The Torana was now available with the 2.8-litre or 3.3-litre 'six'. No V-8s were offered with the new series.

By September 1978 the 1.9-litre, Australian-made Starfire four-cylinder engine had replaced the Sunbird's Opel power plant.

Just over 55 000 UC Sunbirds/Toranas were produced. The hatchback body was discontinued in September 1979. The last Torana was built in December 1979, the last Sunbird in September 1980.

1978 FORD FALCON XC COBRA

The Falcon Cobra, introduced in August 1978, signalled the end of two eras for Ford.

It was the last in a series of two-door Falcons which had started with the 1964 XM Hardtop and it was the last of the high-performance Australian Ford V-8s.

By 1976 Australians had ended their romance with two-door coupes and Ford, like General Motors-Holden's, was looking for an interesting way to dispose of a lot of unused panels.

While GM-H created the luxurious LE Monaro, Ford took another tack and built the high-performance Cobra.

Based on the XC Falcon Hardtop, the Cobra was a boon to those still mourning the 1976 demise of the Falcon GT. The limited run of 400 units included 4.9-litre and 5.75-litre street versions and 30 'Bathurst Specials'.

Available only in white, the new model came with wide blue stripes running along its entire length and Cobra decals on the front guards. The trim was black with blue inserts. Each Cobra was individually numbered on a small dashboard plaque and the figure was repeated in the vehicle serial number.

The standard 4.9-litre Cobra came lavishly equipped with four-wheel power-assisted disc brakes, a limited-slip differential, a dual exhaust system and other features.

The Bathurst models, with a four-speed manual gearbox, had extra equipment including a transmission oil cooling system and twin thermostatically-controlled fans.

In spite of all this, the Cobra was soundly beaten in the 1978 Hardie-Ferodo race. The year before, however, the Falcon Hardtops of Allan Moffat and Colin Bond had figured in a spectacular one-two finish.

1978 GM-H HOLDEN COMMODORE VB

The Holden Commodore sedan was released alongside the larger six-seater HZ model in November 1978.

Though successful enough to quickly become Australia's top-selling car, it never achieved the complete market domination GM-H had hoped for.

The VB Commodore, largely based on a German Opel body design, was launched in three models — Commodore, Commodore SL and Commodore SL/E.

GM-H spent more than $110 million on the new range, hoping to cash in on the trend towards smaller cars sparked by the fuel crisis of the late 1970s. But by the early 1980s, the trend was back to larger cars and in 1982 Ford's Falcon began outselling Holden.

The Commodore used basically the same engine as the 1971 HQ, which was in turn a reworking of the 'red' engine released with the 1963 Holden EH.

Holden utilities and trucks continued on sale using the previous (HZ) body styling until April 1980 when the heavily facelifted WB models appeared. A Commodore wagon appeared shortly after the announcement of the sedan.

The Commodore was *Wheels* magazine's 'Car of the Year' for 1979. It was also very successful in motor sport; Commodores specially prepared by the Holden Dealer Team won the 1979 Repco Round-Australia Trial, the 1980 Australian Touring Car Championship, the 1980 Hardie-Ferodo 1000, the James Hardie 1000 from 1982 to 1984 and scores of other events.

A total of 95 906 VBs were built. □

1978 CHRYSLER VALIANT CM

By 1978 Chrysler was in deep trouble.

Although an all-new Valiant had been ready and waiting for two years, the company did not have the funds to cope with the enormous expense of retooling for it.

As a result, the styling department was again given the job of repackaging the dated, oversized 1971 VH model.

The 'new' CM Valiant — the 13th model Chrysler had extracted from four basic body shapes since 1962 — was announced in November 1978. Identified by a new grille, repackaged tail-lights and varied body mouldings and badges, it carried over all the previous model's body panels.

The CM's big mechanical improvement was that the 'Electronic Lean Burn System' (ELB), an electronic engine management package released on the CL Valiant V-8, had been adapted to suit the six-cylinder Hemi engines. With ELB, the Hemi became much more responsive and Chrysler claimed fuel savings of up to 25 per cent.

The CM range was reduced to three models with the Charger coupe being the major casualty. It was dropped along with the poor-selling panel van and utility.

All CM sedans and wagons incorporated Chrysler's 'Handling Package' (i.e. upgraded suspension). The base-line Valiant was powered by the 245 (4-litre) high-compression Hemi engine with ELB. The more upmarket CM Regal was fitted with a 4.3-litre Hemi 265 engine with ELB, as was a new 'sporty' GLX version of the base Valiant. The top-line CM was the Regal SE. Equipment levels were higher than ever.

Chrysler's main advertising thrust now centred on low purchase price, passenger space and fuel efficiency. The company organised economy tests which showed an excellent 9.4 L/100 km (30 miles per gallon) and better.

When Mitsubishi took over Chrysler's Australian operations in 1980, the factory continued to build Valiants with Chrysler badging. The last came in August 1981. Only 16 005 CMs had been sold in three years.

1979 FORD FALCON XD

Ford Australia spent $102 million preparing the all-new Falcon XD, hoping to produce a strong challenger for Holden's runaway success, the Commodore.

The XD was introduced in March 1979 with a new, smaller body which featured the so-called 'Euro' look. The styling was based on the Ford Granada, although the only common components were the headlights. No two-door model was available.

By providing a more efficient interior layout than the XA/XB/XC series, the new Falcon suffered no reduction in interior space.

The XD was sold with three equipment levels, GL, Fairmont and Fairmont Ghia and with a choice of two six-cylinder engines and two V-8s. The basic unit, the 3.3-litre 'six', developed 82.5 kW; the most powerful, the 5.75-litre V-8, developed 150 kW. New technology in the Falcon design included energy-absorbing urethane bumpers, a polyurethane fuel tank and an electronic cableless speedometer.

The XD was longer, wider, heavier and lower than the Commodore. This was the first time there had been a major difference in size between 'The Big Two' and there was a fiercely fought marketing battle over which size was 'right'. The size difference — and the battle — continued into the late 1980s.

In mid-1980 a Falcon 'XD½' was released with an alloy cylinder head and electronic ignition.

Queensland racing driver Dick Johnson was leading the 1980 Bathurst 1000 in an XD when he hit a rock which had rolled onto the track. Funds provided by a sympathetic public and Ford enabled him to build a winning car for 1981. He won the Australian Touring Car Championship in the same year and again in 1982.

Many XD Falcons were raced and they provided good competition for the Commodores in the traditional 'Ford versus Holden' confrontation.

XD production reached 197 293.

1979 CHRYSLER SIGMA 2.6

The 1977 launch of the GE Sigma sedan enabled Chrysler to take the four-cylinder market by storm.

The Mitsubishi-designed Sigma took only seven months to become the best-selling four-cylinder car in Australia.

Though larger and more expensive, the Sigma was introduced to replace the highly successful Galant. The front-engined/rear-driven newcomer quickly established itself as having an above average standard of finish, and exceptional roadholding and riding comfort for its class.

Furthermore, the equipment levels were high and the styling was considered very modern.

The Sigma was released with three levels of trim: 'Galant', GL and SE. The counter balanced Astron 'Silent Shaft' engine was standard in the GL (1.85-litre) and SE, which had a 2-litre engine.

A GE Wagon was released in 1978 and a sports version, the fully imported Scorpion coupe, was also added to the range.

By 1979 Chrysler had built 50 000 Sigmas and the model was taking 26.7 per cent of its market segment. It did better in 1980 and peaked at 32 per cent in 1981.

1979 saw the release of the locally developed 2.6-litre Astron engine. This large and powerful four-cylinder engine further boosted the Sigma's appeal.

Despite the success of the Sigma, Chrysler Australia was in dire trouble, as was its parent company in the US.

In April 1980 Mitsubishi completely bought out Chrysler Australia (for a total of $77 million) and on 1 October that year the name was changed to Mitsubishi Motors Australia Ltd. The new firm immediately announced ambitious expansion plans.

The GH Sigma, released April 1980, was the last to wear a Chrysler badge, but Sigma remained a best-seller.□

1979 FORD FAIRLANE ZJ

In May 1979, Ford took the unusual step of releasing an all-new Fairlane that wasn't bigger than the previous one.

The ZJ Fairlane, which was based on the XD Falcon, was lighter, shorter and narrower than the ZH model it replaced. Despite this, space efficiency was greatly improved and leg-room was increased.

The base ZJ had a 4.9-litre V-8 engine with a three-speed automatic transmission. It had a horizontal grille — providing the so-called 'Mercedes look' — and twin, square headlamps set above an energy-absorbing bumper.

The LTD, once the larger and more upmarket version dubbed the 'Canberra Special' (because of its use by politicians), now shared the same wheelbase and body panels.

Late in 1979 six-cylinder versions of the Fairlane and LTD were introduced to combat a decline in sales caused by the fuel crisis.

The distinctive two-toned Fairlane Sportsman was unveiled in October 1980 with alloy road wheels and a choice between a 4.1-litre 'six' and a 4.9-litre V-8. In March 1982 Fairlane and LTD were given a coil spring and Watt's linkage rear suspension set-up and additional interior equipment. They also received a new grille and tail-lamp assemblies.

Fuel-injection became available on both Fairlane and LTD in February 1983. By this stage the V-8 was no longer sold.

The Fairlane and LTD were still in production in the mid-1980s with minor revisions to the exterior. By 1985 they were available with electronic features such as a trip computer, digital instrumentation, electronic cruise control, power windows, power door locks, climate control air-conditioning and motorised air vents.

1980 GM-H HOLDEN COMMODORE VC

The facelifted Commodore VC range was announced in April 1980 and, by the end of the year, it offered buyers a four-cylinder engine in addition to the 'six' and V-8.

The four-cylinder model, released in June, was not popular in Australia but recorded big sales in New Zealand, where it was subject to much less tax due to its smaller engine capacity.

The 1.8-litre 'four' was based on the Holden Sunbird's Starfire engine with a different camshaft and carburettor to improve the fuel economy and quietness. The general feeling among traditional Holden buyers, however, was that the Commodore 'four' had too little power for its weight.

The six-cylinder and eight-cylinder engines offered with the VC (which proved far more popular) were revised 'XT5' versions, which were up to 25 per cent more powerful and 15 per cent more economical than the previous engines. This was achieved with a redesigned cylinder head, camshaft, carburettor, inlet manifold and exhaust manifold plus electronic ignition and a reduced compression ratio.

The VC range reintroduced 'shadow tone' paint work — something that hadn't been seen on a new Holden for 20 years.

In 1980 the last full-sized family Holden — an HZ Kingswood — came off the production line. During 1979 over 20 000 HZ Kingswoods had been sold. This success persuaded GM-H to design a 'WB' Kingswood based on the Statesman wheelbase, but the plan to produce this was halted at the last moment.

In June 1981 the four-millionth Holden, a VC sedan, was built. Commodore continued as Australia's top-selling car; total output of VC sedans and wagons amounted to 109 231.

1980 SPANMOR LTD

Australia's longest passenger car, an extended wheelbase Ford LTD, is the product of a Melbourne-based specialist coachbuilder aptly named Spanmor.

Released in 1980, the Spanmor LTD is over six metres long. It has seating for up to nine (depending on choice of interior layout) and features a host of luxury equipment never before offered in an Australian car. This includes a refrigerator, dual air-conditioning system and divider with intercom. Options comprise a phone, colour TV, video, moon roof, cocktail bar and virtually anything else the buyer specifies.

In line with the popular American 'stretched' luxury sedans, the Spanmor maintains the standard LTD mechanical components. Spanmor also builds ambulances, funeral vehicles and security cars.

1980 HDT COMMODORE

The 'Brock' Commodore, as this car was quickly dubbed, is a highly modified version of the locally-built Holden Commodore V-8.

Produced by HDT Special Vehicles Pty Ltd, under the directorship of Australia's most successful touring car racing driver, Peter Brock, the HDT Commodore revived the 'muscle' car which had been so popular in the late 1960s and early 1970s.

Sometimes called 'Australia's sixth-biggest car maker', HDT Special Vehicles has received close cooperation from General Motors-Holden's. By 1982 it was producing about 400 Commodores per year, featuring a variety of performance and accessory options.

Victorian-born Peter Brock started racing in a Holden-powered Austin A30 in 1967. His outstanding ability led to his signing with the Holden Dealer Team and he soon became its number one driver. By 1986 he had taken a record eight wins in the annual Bathurst production car endurance race, had won the Australian Touring Car Championship three times and also gained scores of titles in racing, rallying, rallycross and other branches of motor sport.

In 1980 Brock bought the Holden Dealer Team organisation and started marketing modified Holden V-8 Commodores for racing and road use.

The original HDT Commodore was followed by the highly successful SS Commodore, SS Group Three Commodore, and top-of-the-line Calais Director. 550 SS Group A Commodores were made in 1985 to comply with worldwide homologation regulations for Group A Touring Car racing.

In early 1986, HDT Special Vehicles produced its first six-cylinder car, a version of the VL series Holden Calais LE, then followed with a turbocharged version.

A new 'Group A' V-8 was unveiled in September 1986 at the Sydney Motor Show. □

1980 GM-H STATESMAN WB

Despite some vigorous marketing, GM-H was never able to seriously challenge Ford's Fairlane with the upmarket Statesman.

The WB versions of the Statesman de Ville and the Statesman Caprice were launched in 1980, by which time the Holden design on which they were based had been replaced by the Commodore.

Although it incorporated a few carryover body panels from the previous Statesman, the new top-of-the-line Holden had a completely new look. It also boasted increased interior space, an all-new interior and an improved version of Holden's 5-litre V-8.

An even longer list of standard equipment was fitted. The Caprice was the first Australian-made car to be equipped with a cruise control system as standard; it also had power windows, central door locking, a four-speaker sound system and other equipment. Leather trim was optional.

The WB range included utility, panel van and cab/chassis models based on the previous Kingswood designs.

The Statesman Series II was released in September 1983 with de Ville and Caprice levels of equipment. Changes were cosmetic but it was now the only local V-8-powered car on the market.

HDT Special Vehicles produced the Magnum, a high-performance version of the Statesman de Ville, with an engine developing 188 kW.

At the end of 1984, GM-H announced it was vacating the big-car field to concentrate on luxury versions of the smaller Commodore.

1981 DATSUN BLUEBIRD

Launched in May 1981, Bluebird was the car that finally knocked the Chrysler/Mitsubishi Sigma off the top of the four-cylinder sales charts.

Promoted by a curious advertising campaign describing it as 'the world's first four-cylinder limousine', the Bluebird was a reasonably conventional Datsun using most of the mechanical components fitted to the previous 200B model.

Nevertheless, it was a much-improved vehicle with modern styling, generous interior room and a wide range of options and equipment levels. Much praised at the time of its release, within weeks Bluebird wrested four-cylinder class leadership from Sigma.

From the outset the Bluebird had 85 per cent local content. Model revisions were made in 1982 and again in 1983, when it was renamed the Nissan Bluebird in line with the Japanese corporate policy. A total of 130 000 Bluebirds were made at Clayton, Victoria, between 1981 and early 1986, when production ceased to make way for the Pintara and Skyline models.

'Bluebird' is a stalwart Nissan name. In 1959 the company exhibited a Datsun Bluebird at the Melbourne Motor Show. Soon after, former GM-H chief executive Larry (later Sir Laurence) Hartnett imported a shipment of 1.3-litre models.

In 1977 the first locally built Datsun — the 200B — was produced. In 1981 the Bluebird name was reinstated and, in 1984, the 100 000th Bluebird came out of the Clayton plant.

Nissan used two turbocharged Bluebirds in a spirited campaign to win the 1981 James Hardie 1000. Although outright victory eluded the company, Nissan went on to win the 1982 Australian Endurance Championship of Makes.

By the end of 1986, a Bluebird (driven by George Fury) still held the outright record for the fastest lap by a touring car at Bathurst. It had been achieved during qualifying for the 1984 James Hardie 1000.

1981 GM-H HOLDEN COMMODORE VH

The VH range continued the refinement of Holden's Commodore series.

Launched in October 1981, it comprised five models, with five engine options and four transmissions (including the first five-speed manual gearbox).

The body style remained basically the same but a longer, lower frontal appearance was introduced.

The four-cylinder version was retained (in spite of heavy criticism) alongside the 'sixes' and eight-cylinder models.

Such amenities as climate control air-conditioning and cruise control were offered in an extremely long options list. A feature of the SL/E model was GM-H's first trip computer.

For a number of reasons, including poor judgment on new model designs and intense competition, GM-H's share of the market was continuing to fall. What had been a 50 per cent share of the market in the golden days of the late 1950s, was progressively reduced to 34 per cent in 1968 and 25.5 per cent in 1975. By 1983, when the VH was still in production, it had tumbled to 18 per cent.

During the early 1980s, GM-H lost hundreds of millions of dollars and was forced to completely restructure its operation. A major recovery plan, announced in 1983, included the closure of some major plants and the purchasing of more components (and later complete cars!) from overseas. Part of the fightback was centred around the restyled VK Commodore, which was being prepared for release in early 1984.

Despite GM-H's marketing problems, great things were happening on the racetrack. Commodore blitzed the Touring Car class with a string of victories which included first outright at the annual Bathurst 1000 kilometre touring car race in 1980, 1982, 1983, 1984 and 1986.

126 823 VHs were sold.

1982 MITSUBISHI COLT RB

Big things were expected of the RB Colt.

It was based on the front-drive four-door Japanese Colt hatchback, a model first imported to Australia in late 1980.

Inability to keep up with demand for the imported Colt led to the decision by Mitsubishi Motors Australia Limited to produce the car at its Tonsley Park (Adelaide) plant.

In 1982 the local RB series Colt rolled off MMAL's production line. Fitted with an unusual dual-range transmission, it was available in 1.4-litre and 1.6-litre versions.

The new Colt was well received but the big sales Mitsubishi Motors Australia Limited had expected did not eventuate.

The facelifted RC was released in 1984 with a sedan version added to the range.

The Colt continued to be built in small numbers during 1985 and 1986 but, by then, MMAL was concentrating on supplying the overwhelming demand for the bigger Magna.□

1982 FORD FALCON XE

1982 was a milestone year for Ford Australia — the year Falcon finally became Australia's number one selling car.

Until then the best Falcon had done was to lead the Holden for a few months at a time — never a whole year.

By 1982 'big' was no longer a dirty word and buyers were moving back to the traditional-sized Australian car. Ford was perfectly placed with Falcon while GM-H, locked into building the smaller Holden Commodore, was losing ground.

In March 1982 the facelifted Falcon XE was announced. Based on the previous XD, it had an new aerodynamically styled wrapover bonnet and a coil spring suspension set-up replacing the former leaf springs.

November 1982 saw the discontinuation of the Falcon V-8 engines, due to a decision made at a time when there was a swing away from big engines. Ford compensated by offering fuel-injection for the 'six' in early 1983. This lifted the power of the 4.1-litre engine by 15 kW.

After the V-8s were dropped, the engine choice was between the 3.3-litre, and 4.1-litre, six-cylinder engines. For the first time, Ford offered a five-speed manual gearbox.

The XE was available in sedan, wagon, panel van and utility form.

By the time of the XE's release, the Chrysler Valiant had been discontinued. Holden's Commodore was a composite of local engineering and Opel design, and Ford was the only company with a family car designed and built in Australia.

Falcon's climb to the top had been a long process. By 1981 Falcon was consistently outselling Holden and would have taken the lead but for a factory strike. In 1982 Ford vehicles finally outsold GM-H vehicles for an entire year.

To compound the sales success, Dick Johnson drove a Falcon XE to win the 1984 Australian Touring Car Championship.

191 209 XEs were sold.□

1982 MITSUBISHI SIGMA GJ

The 1982 all-new GJ Sigma was a big surprise.

The much-awaited all-new body was so similar to the previous one that people had to look twice to realise there was anything different.

As well as having every outer panel changed, the GJ Sigma incorporated a large number of engineering improvements. It used the same engines, however, as the previous series.

A 2-litre Mitsubishi GH Sigma Turbo, Australia's first turbocharged production sedan, was released late in 1981. It was not successful and plans to produce a turbocharged car using the new body were shelved.

By 1983 Sigma had lost market leadership in the four-cylinder class but was still selling well to private and fleet buyers. The Sigma wagon remained Australia's top-selling wagon.

The 250 000th Australian-built Sigma, a GK, rolled off the Tonsley Park (Adelaide) production line in 1984. A high-roof wagon was released in 1985 and production of this and the sedan continued right through 1986.

By this time Mitsubishi was producing three local models (Magna, Sigma and Colt) and importing a range of highly acclaimed cars and light commercial vehicles.□

1982 GM-H HOLDEN CAMIRA JB

Camira — the Australian version of General Motors world 'J Car' — was the first front-wheel drive car built by GM-H.

Launched in July 1982 with a 1.6-litre, four-cylinder 'Camtech 4' engine, Camira was initially built only as a sedan. It came with a four-speed gearbox and optional automatic transmission.

The original model Camira was designated the JB. A five-door wagon version came in April 1983; this was the first 'J-car' wagon variant designed outside the US.

To supply the Camira's engine, GM-H built a new plant with a potential output of 300 000 units per year, with a view to exporting two-thirds of its production (mainly to Europe). The company then became Australia's largest exporter of manufactured goods, with export sales of $1 million a day.

The Camira won many plaudits, including the respected *Wheels* magazine's 'Car of the Year' award for 1982.

Despite its brilliant design, the Camira suffered build-quality problems and was not the enormous sales success that GM-H had hoped for.

1982 CANSTEL CLUBMAN

The Canstel Clubman is one of the most successful local specialist sports cars. Forty were built from 1968 to 1973 by Specialised Fibreglass Mouldings. The car was then made under licence by GS Motor Bodies Pty Ltd of Carlton, NSW, and total production neared 100 units. The Canstel was designed to be suitable for road use and club racing. It incorporated a modified Triumph Herald chassis and all-independent suspension. The most popular power unit was a Ford 1.6-litre engine.

The car was usually sold in kit form but at various times (including the 1980s), fully built-up models were available.

1983 GM-H HOLDEN GEMINI TG ZZ/Z

The Gemini was first released in Australia as the TX model in 1975.

It was a true international, combining German design, Japanese mechanicals and Australian assembly. Local content crept up over the years and the Gemini was styled to look like its 'big brother', the full-sized Holden.

Initially, Gemini was available in sedan and coupe form.

It soon became Australia's most popular four-cylinder car and stayed at the top until the Chrysler/Mitsubishi Sigma cleaned up the market in the late 1970s and early 1980s.

A minor revision of the original design brought about the Gemini TC in January 1977.

The TD Gemini was released in March 1978 and included the luxury SL/E version, a two-door station wagon and a two-door panel van.

Late 1979 brought the TE range. This was expanded in 1981 to include a 1.8-litre diesel sedan with a five-speed gearbox. Coupe styles were dropped; the Gypsy panel van was released.

The TG, released March 1983, brought many refinements and introduced the ZZ/Z sedan.

The ZZ/Z model took its name from the Japanese 'ZZ' Gemini, a high-performance version fitted with a 1.8-litre double overhead cam engine. Unfortunately, the name was all the Australian-built version borrowed. Despite the large number of stripes, decals and sports fittings, the ZZ/Z used the standard 1.6-litre power plant, albeit coupled to a five-speed manual gearbox.

A front-drive Gemini was assembled in Australia from May 1985. It was virtually identical to the car sold in the US and Japan.□

1983 TOYOTA CORONA

Toyota announced its first Australian-built Corona in June 1983.

It was a completely new design, unique to Australia, and made in four-door sedan and five-door wagon versions.

Powered by an imported 2-litre, four-cylinder engine, it had 25 per cent more power than its predecessor, which used a 1.9-litre Holden-made engine. The Corona was the first Australian-built car to offer a four-speed automatic transmission.

The medium-sized rear-drive Corona had been introduced to Australia as a fully imported model in 1964. By 1965 local assembly (by AMI) commenced to provide a replacement for the Toyota Tiara. In 1966 AMI began increasing the local content and added imported wagon and fastback variants. In 1968 the 30 000th Corona came off AMI's assembly line.

A new-look Corona arrived in 1971, followed a year later by the Corona Mark II with a six-cylinder engine. In 1974 the restyled Corona with a 2-litre engine went into production.

Meanwhile, Toyota sales continued strongly. By 1973 the company had sold 200 000 cars downunder.

By March 1976 the Corona had 85 per cent local content. Fifteen months after the release of the first Australian Corona in 1983, the model was further improved when a 2.4-litre Avante engine became available.

By this stage AMI-Toyota Ltd was importing a large number of models and fully manufacturing a range of 'Australianised' Toyota Corollas. □

1983 PERENTTI

The spectacular Perentti sports car was designed and built by Revolution Fibreglass Pty Ltd in Melbourne.

Introduced at the Sydney Motor Show in 1983, the two-door Perentti coupe was at first sold as a kit car and then later marketed in finished form.

Styled with the Chevrolet Corvette as its main influence, the Perentti is based on a Holden panel van chassis and uses Holden components throughout.

The design features two-plus-two seating, a T-bar roof, a large luggage area and a choice between a six-cylinder and a V-8 engine. The vehicle is built with steel intrusion bars in the doors and body panels and was designed to conform to 1983 Australian Design Rules standards.

A slightly updated 'Mark II' version was released in 1986.

Revolution Fibreglass P/L also builds the Ferrari Dino-influenced Condor body for VW chassis as well as dress-up kits and spoilers for production cars.

1984 GM-H HOLDEN COMMODORE VK

By the time Commodore's VK range came in February 1984, Falcon was Australia's top-selling car.

GM-H's financial troubles were well publicised and it was obvious the company had to hit back hard.

The VK was the weapon. It had extensive styling changes but maintained the same basic body shape. Most importantly, it featured electronic fuel-injection and a computerised engine management system. Performance was improved but without loss of fuel economy.

There was an enormous amount of other additional equipment, yet the VK was actually cheaper than the previous VH model.

The VK series introduced new model names: SL, Berlina and Calais. The Calais, which was top-of-the-line, was fitted with an Australian-made digital/analog electronic instrument panel claimed to be the most advanced in the world.

The most significant changes to the Commodore's appearance since its release were effected by six-window styling and a louvered grille which was integrated with a moulded polypropylene bumper.

The VK didn't win back total market leadership but, in the second half of 1984, Holden outsold Falcon for the first time in two years.

1984 NISSAN PULSAR TURBO ET

The Pulsar Turbo ET was the first locally made turbocharged car to record big sales.

With dazzling performance for a car of its size and price, the small four-door hatchback cut its own niche in the marketplace.

Powered by a 1.5-litre, four-cylinder engine coupled to a five-speed manual gearbox, the front-drive ET accelerates from rest to 100 km/h in under ten seconds and covers the standing 400 metres in 16.5 seconds.

The normally aspirated Nissan Pulsar, on which the turbo was based, came here as the fully imported Datsun Pulsar in 1980. It was the company's first front-wheel drive car sold in Australia. Pulsar was later locally manufactured with a choice of 1.3-litre and 1.5-litre engines.

In September 1983 a fully imported two-door 1.5-litre turbo coupe was added to the range; in April 1984 the locally built Pulsar Turbo ET hatchback was released.

Nissan scored an industry triumph in 1984 by selling the front-drive Pulsar to General Motors-Holden's, which marketed the Pulsar as the Holden Astra (in normally aspirated form only).

The Pulsar had originally been sold as a Datsun; in 1983 Nissan of Japan made the decision to discontinue the name Datsun worldwide and call all future models by the corporate name of Nissan.

1984 WASP

The unusual Wasp was an exciting concept, in some ways capturing the spirit of early three-wheeled sports cars like Morgan and BSA.

Produced by Autocycle Engineering and displayed at the 1984 Sydney International Motor Show, the fibreglass-bodied machine combined a small car-type body and steering system with a motorcycle drive train and rear wheel.

The Wasp was claimed to combine the power, reliability and economy of a motorcycle with sports car handling, comfort and style. The company offered the vehicle with a choice of motorcycle drivetrains; the top-of-the-line was 110 kilowatts in power.

Unfortunately the cost of the Wasp was high and few were sold.□

1984 TRIAD

The spectacular Triad, a Sydney-built sports coupe, was claimed to be one of the strongest and safest cars ever built.

After 30 months of designing and testing, a prototype was exhibited in 1984. Limited production was announced at a cost of $50 000 per car but by the end of 1986 this had still not started.

The mid-engined two-seater was powered by a 2.8-litre Volvo V-6 engine developing 115 kW and was claimed to have a top speed of 225 km/h.

The Triad was conceived by former Ford engineer Cliff Trefry and the prototype was constructed by former Rolls-Royce coachbuilders Wally and Bobby Hadley, using fibreglass and Kevlar body panels.

Features included four-wheel independent suspension, air-conditioning, an elaborate sound system and a cockpit fully trimmed in leather.

The Triad weighs 1020 kg, with 48 per cent of the weight on the front wheels.

1984 FORD FALCON XF

By 1984 Ford Australia was calling the shots as market leader.

Not only did it have the number one selling car, the Falcon, but Ford also marketed a whole range of successful Japanese-sourced small and medium-sized vehicles, making it the most profitable car company in Australia.

In October 1984 the Falcon XF model was announced. A further refinement of the XD/XE series, it had new front body panels with a 'softened' (more rounded) nose and new-look tail-lights. A completely new interior included such items as a fold-down rear seat centre-flap, stereo tape player and digital clock as standard.

Although styling changes were minor, there were marked engineering improvements. Power was lifted and fuel economy improved, mainly due to Ford USA's EEC 4 electronic engine management system and a higher lift camshaft.

Due to its tie-in with Mazda in Japan, Ford was able to offer a host of improvements to Falcon's electronics. The upmarket Ghia was now available with a 12-function trip computer, digital instrumentation (with systems test panel), motorized dashboard air vents, electronic cruise control and climate control air-conditioning.

Ford's passenger-car-derived utilities and panel vans were now the only full-size vehicles of their type, following a decision by Holden to vacate the market.

Ford Australia maintained the number one spot during 1983, 1984 and 1985, building its 1.5-millionth Falcon along the way.

At the start of 1986, the compulsory change was made to unleaded petrol. Holden announced the VL model with a new, more powerful and more economical engine; Ford made do with a modified (and less powerful) version of its existing power plant. Although Ford maintained its overall market leadership for most of the year, the margin was reduced.

The unleaded version of the XF Falcon is identified by a small 'repeater' light fitted to the front bumper bar surrounds.

1984 GM-H HOLDEN CAMIRA JD

The Camira JD — launched in November 1984 — was a refinement and further 'Australianisation' of General Motors' world 'J Car'.

Introduced two and a half years after the original JB series, the JD had a significantly new look and offered an optional 1.8-litre engine fitted with Bosch fuel-injection.

The fuel-injected engine boosted power by 30 per cent, transforming a fairly uninspired performer into an exceptionally sprightly car.

New features included variable rate front shock absorbers with rerated rear springs for a softer ride, a digital electronic ignition advance system and multifocal headlamps.

The new front-end body design improved aerodynamics and gave the car a distinctive look, later borrowed by Camira's 'big brother', the Holden Commodore.

The press reaction was almost unanimous — the JD was a much better car than the JB.

Unfortunately the compulsory switch to unleaded fuel in 1986 robbed the revitalised Camira of much of its additional power. Sales slumped.

1985 MITSUBISHI MAGNA

Few cars have been as well received as Mitsubishi's Magna.

Released in early 1985, the completely new front-drive sedan won virtually every media 'Car Of The Year' award and sold so quickly that Mitsubishi's Tonsley Park factory was expanded to keep up with demand.

Longer and wider than the big-selling Mitsubishi Sigma, the Magna is powered by the Australian-developed 2.6-litre Astron engine, mounted east-west and driving the front wheels. The model quickly became the company's main thrust into the Australian market and was the first four-cylinder car to effectively compete against the established 'sixes'.

The Magna was developed from the Japanese 'Galant Sigma' but was widened by Australian engineers and fitted with the local power train. It was introduced in GLX, SE and luxury 'Elite' form.

Mitsubishi Motors Australia Limited was formed in October 1980 when Mitsubishi bought the ailing Chrysler Australia operations. The Magna was the first full-sized family car from the company since the Valiant was phased out in 1981.

MMAL spent $60 million developing the new model. With losses in the three years preceding its release, the Magna was widely thought to be the make-or-break car for the company's local operations.

But strong sales were recorded from the outset.

At the end of 1985, the Astron engine was modified to run on unleaded fuel. In September 1986 an 'Executive' variant was released, aimed at business fleets.

By late 1986 over 50 000 Magnas had been built.

1985 FORD LASER TURBO

Ford's decision to switch from Europe to Japan as the source of its small and medium-sized family cars led to the introduction of the Laser, Telstar and Meteor models.

All were based on Mazda designs and locally assembled using local and imported parts.

In June 1985 Ford Australia catered for the trend towards small turbocharged cars by building the limited edition Laser Turbo.

Pitched against the locally built Nissan ET Turbo, Ford's five-door hatchback rocket was developed in conjunction with the Sydney company, Turbocharger Technology.

Using the basic 1.5-litre Laser engine coupled to a Solex 32DIS carburettor and turbocharger, Ford produced an extremely lively small car.

As well as the increased power and torque (78 kW and 157 Nm), the Turbo incorporated the suspension package developed by Ford Australia for the normally aspirated Laser Sport model. Other refinements, such as low-profile Pirelli P6 tyres, Recaro seats and a colour-keyed all-white exterior finish made the Laser Turbo a sought-after model.

Geared for maximum performance between 0 and 100 km/h rather than a high top speed, the Laser Turbo could do the standing 400 metres in 17.1 seconds. That is only a fraction slower than the original Falcon GT, powered by a 4.7-litre V-8!

The Turbo version was dropped when the all-new Laser was introduced in late 1985.

1986 GM-H HOLDEN COMMODORE VL

The first major styling and mechanical changes to Holden's Commodore came with the controversial VL model in February 1986.

The VL featured a completely new front-end appearance and was powered by an imported Nissan six-cylinder engine.

The new model was much criticised — many thought it sacrilege to give 'Australia's own car' a Japanese power plant. After driving the VL, however, most critics agreed that the new 3-litre engine was the best 'six' yet seen in a Holden or any other Australian-built car.

While Ford had made the compulsory switch to unleaded fuel (in January 1986) by fitting the Falcon with a sedated version of the old engine, Holden was able to announce a Commodore with 33 per cent more power and 15 per cent better fuel economy than before.

Among the features in the state-of-the-art engine was a self-diagnostic module designed to detect and memorise mechanical faults.

The engine was one of several improvements. There were new four-speed automatic and five-speed manual transmissions (also from Nissan), different interior trim and a redesigned instrument panel. A small air foil was integrated into the boot lid.

For the first time, the top-of-the-line Holden, the Calais, had significantly different styling to the rest of the range. Its front-end treatment made use of semiconcealed headlights.

In the second half of 1986, a turbocharger was introduced as an option across the range. This turned the already sprightly Commodore into a genuine 'supercar', capable of accelerating to 100 km/h in eight seconds and reaching a top speed of 220 km/h.

Later in the year, the locally made 4.9-litre V-8 (now modified for unleaded fuel) was re-released as an option.

After the initial controversy, the VL was warmly received. In April 1986 Holden hit the top of the sales charts, and although this lead was not maintained through 1986, Holden's market share was the best for a long time.

1986 TOYOTA COROLLA TWIN CAM

The sensational Toyota Corolla Twin Cam was released in early 1986, powered by the first locally-made twin overhead camshaft engine.

With an 86 kW power plant coupled to a five-speed gearbox, it was easily the fastest-accelerating 1.6-litre normally aspirated Australia production car released to that date.

The Corolla Twin Cam was based on the front-wheel drive Toyota Corolla which was launched in 1985, replacing a string of successful rear-wheel drive Corollas.

The front-drive Corolla was initially available with a choice of a 1.3-litre engine or an optional 1.6-litre unit. Body styles included sedan and liftback versions with a hatchback added later.

The Twin Cam was released as a hatchback and slightly larger Seca liftback. Engineered in Altona (Melbourne), the 1.6-litre 'hot hatch' can charge to 100 km/h in under ten seconds and reach nearly 200 km/h in fifth gear. It can cover the standing 400 metres in under 17 seconds.

The Corolla was introduced to Australia in 1967 as a fully imported vehicle and was assembled in Melbourne from 1968. By March 1976 the Corolla was locally built and boasted local design input.

By the 1980s AMI/Toyota was also manufacturing the 'Australianised' Corona.

1986 NISSAN PINTARA

Based on the Japanese Nissan Skyline but locally built with a significant Australian design content, the four-cylinder Pintara was introduced in mid-1986.

It replaced the Bluebird and carried the hopes of local car maker Nissan Australia in the highly-competitive four-cylinder market.

A four-door sedan and five-door wagon were offered. The Pintara was fitted with an Australian-made, fuel-injected, 2-litre engine with twin spark plugs and a cross-flow cylinder head. It featured a high level of standard equipment including four-wheel disc brakes, power mirrors, tachometer and stereo sound system.

Buyers had the choice between a five-speed manual and a four-speed automatic transmission with electronic overdrive.

Pintara represented a move upmarket for Nissan, with its dearer price tag and heavy accent on quality, reliability and durability. The release came at a time when imported car prices were rising sharply and Nissan Australia boasted that it would win over many buyers who could no longer afford imported cars.

A six-cylinder 'Skyline' version of the Pintara was released in July 1986 (see separate entry). □

1986 TD 2000

Looks can deceive. The TD 2000 is both modern and Australian.

Powered by a locally built 2-litre Nissan engine (as used in the Nissan Pintara) and using Nissan running gear, the TD 2000 represents one of the most ambitious local car-building projects ever undertaken.

The TD 2000 was conceived by former Mercedes-dealer Ross Marshall and more than $3 million was spent on its development, testing and tooling. Marshall announced that his company was aiming at a production run of 12 000 units a year for sale worldwide.

Built in Victoria for the Australian market and in Taiwan (using Australian components) for the rest of the world, the TD 2000 was widely exhibited in 1986. Delays, however, led to the company postponing the release until 1987.

Although based on the 1949-1953 MG TD design, the TD 2000 is 60 mm wider and has been designed to suit all major world markets. It has passed strict Australian and US safety and emission standards.

The modern TD uses fibreglass body panels made by Bolwell. 1980s creature comforts include modern switchgear, instrumentation and a stereo sound sytem. A roll bar and seat belts are fitted, as is a sophisticated burglar alarm.

With a five-speed gearbox and a power-to-weight ratio of about twice that of the original MG TD, the TD 2000 combines modern sports car performance with 'square-rigger' appearance.□

1986 NISSAN SKYLINE 'TI'

1986 was 'The Year of The Skyline' for Nissan Australia.

While the Skyline coupe conquered all on Australian race circuits, 48 Australian motoring journalists elected the Skyline sedan as *Modern Motor* magazine's 'Car of The Year'.

The Skyline sedan/wagon range was announced in July 1986, powered by a high-tech, 3-litre, six-cylinder Nissan engine similar to that fitted to Holden's 1986 VL Commodore.

Like the four-cylinder Pintara, the Skyline was based on the Japanese Nissan Skyline but locally built with increased body strengthening and other Australian-engineered changes. The Pintara replaced an existing model, the Bluebird, but the Skyline took the company into the high-volume six-cylinder market for the first time, putting it in direct competition with Holden and Falcon.

Although criticised for its 'boxy' styling, the Skyline was much praised for its high standards of finish and exceptional structural strength. It featured a high level of standard equipment and offered a choice between a five-speed manual and a four-speed automatic transmission.

The highly-successful Skyline race car was based on the Japanese coupe, but was developed in Sydney. With lightweight construction and a 2-litre turbocharged engine, it proved extremely quick and reliable and won more major Australian touring car races during 1986 than any other car.

A 'Ti' version of the Australian Skyline sedan was released late in 1986. Although mechanically similar to other Skyline models, it offered a more luxurious interior and a higher equipment level. It was a big sales success.

The sales revival which followed the launch of the new models could not have been more welcome. Nissan Australia had looked in bad shape in 1985 and early 1986, with sales and market share dropping month by month.

In spite of a disasterous year for the motoring industry in 1986, Nissan finished strongly and, with the announcement of the 'Car Of The Year' award, the company found a new impetus.□

1986 FORD FALCON 'XF½' GHIA WAGON

In October 1986 Ford announced an upgraded Falcon.

In the face of new competition from the Nissan Skyline, Holden Commodore V-8 and Holden Commodore Turbo and the continuing success of the Mitsubishi Magna, Ford gave the entire Falcon line-up an improved equipment level and a new colour-keyed appearance.

Widely referred to as the 'XF½' (although simply described by Ford Australia as the 1987 Falcon), the revision gave all Falcons colour-keyed grilles, rocker panels and bumper bars.

Four-wheel disc brakes and power steering became standard although Ford said that owners could specify manual steering if they wished. The XF½ Falcon also brought trim changes and other minor alterations. An optional five-speed transmission was announced but the engines — the 3.3-litre 'six' and 4.1-litre 'six' — remained the same as when modified in early 1986 to suit unleaded petrol.

The Falcon model range was expanded to include a luxurious 'Ghia' version of the station wagon.

With its slightly more modern appearance, Falcon stayed at the top of the sales chart in the final months of 1986 and finished the year with overall sales nearly 12 000 ahead of its nearest rival, the Holden Commodore.

The 'XF½' was the fourth repackaging of the XD Falcon in the eight years since its release. While the marketing men at Ford kept at the job of selling the long-in-the-tooth Falcon, the engineers continued working on the all-new model (code-named the 'EA26') expected in 1988.

1986 CHIMERA

The Chimera represents an ambitious Sydney attempt to launch a high-performance grand touring coupe.

The vehicle, which takes its name from a mythical fire-spouting monster, has been a long-term project of sports and racing car builder Henry Nehrybecki.

He started designing the vehicle in 1977 and built the first prototype in 1980. Work was still underway in 1986 at a small factory at Hornsby (Sydney). By then two cars were completed but Nehrybecki was awaiting overseas funds before continuing.

The Chimera incorporates many racing car features but has a liftback body with seating for four. Nehrybecki believes he can sell up to 50 per year in Australia and 500 in the US once full production is underway.

The Chimera body is made from alloy and Kevlar and incorporates a space frame and roll cage. Power comes from a twin-turbocharged 3.8-litre GM V-6 engine driving a five-speed manual transmission (or four-speed automatic), with MacPherson strut suspension on all wheels and rack-and-pinion steering.

The car uses many Nehrybecki-designed mechanical parts including the rear suspension. A 4WD version is also planned.

1986 TAIPAN

With a lightweight fibreglass body, 7.4-litre twin-turbocharged V-8 and 'cannon-proof' drive line, the Taipan is easily the fastest in a long line of Aussie performance cars.

Styled on the Anglo-American AC/Shelby Cobra of the 1960s, but designed and built by the Sydney-based GJM company, the Taipan went on sale in December 1986.

By that time, three had been completed and the company was engaged in building five more.

According to Geoff McHattan, the man behind the project, the Taipan is virtually the only Cobra replica to equal or better the awesome performance which put the original '427' Cobra in the *Guinness Book of Records*.

Calling the Taipan 'the fastest street-legal car ever available in Australia' the GJM company issued performance figures which gave the 0 to 100 km/h time as four seconds and claimed a 12.9 seconds standing 400 metres. This compares with 6.4 and 14.3 seconds for a Ferrari 328 GTB/GTS.

The Taipan's 7.4-litre engine is based on a Chevrolet block, with a special cylinder head and twin turbochargers. It runs on LPG (which McHattan says produces more power than unleaded fuel) and develops about 300 kW.

Four-wheel disc brakes and rack-and-pinion steering are fitted.

At the time of the Taipan's release, McHattan said: 'We understand that, statistically, our chances of success [as a specialist sports car maker] are minimal'. Soon afterwards he reported that he had received a large number of inquiries from potential buyers.

INDEX
(AUSSIE CARS LISTED WITH DATES)

AAM 1929 — 58
ACE 1904 — 32
ACME 1916 — 46
ALBANI SIX 1922 — 53
ANDERSON 1906 — 37
ASCORT 1958 — 73
AUSCAR 1938 — 62
AUSTIN LANCER 1958 — 76
AUSTIN FREEWAY 1962 — 84
AUSTIN X6 KIMBERLY 1970 — 116
AUSTRAL 1913 — 44
AUSTRALIA 1904 — 32
AUSTRALIAN FOUR 1912 — 41
AUSTRALIAN SIX 1919 — 48
AUSTRALIS 1906 — 36

B & B 1913 — 41
BASSIN 1950 — 66
BATEUP 1939 — 62
BESST SUPER FOUR 1925 — 55
BOLWELL NAGARI 1970 — 115
BUCHANAN COBRA 1958 — 77
BUCKINGHAM 1933 — 58
BUCKLE 1956 — 69
BULLOCK 1902 — 24

CALDWELL-VALE 1913 — 42
CAMPBELL 1900 — 20
CANSTEL CLUBMAN 1982 — 169

CARTER 1920 — 50
CHIC 1923 — 54
CHIMERA 1986 — 187

CHRYSLER CENTURA KB 1975 — 141
CHRYSLER 'CHRYSLER' 1971 — 126
CHRYSLER SIGMA 2.6 1979 — 157
CHRYSLER VALIANT R SERIES 1962 — 82
CHRYSLER VALIANT S SERIES 1962 — 85
CHRYSLER VALIANT AP5 1963 — 88
CHRYSLER VALIANT AP6 1965 — 94
CHRYSLER VALIANT VC 1966 — 96
CHRYSLER VALIANT VE 1967 — 101
CHRYSLER VALIANT VF 1969 — 106
CHRYSLER VALIANT VG 1970 — 112
CHRYSLER VALIANT VH 1971 — 119
CHRYSLER VALIANT GALANT 1971 — 127
CHRYSLER VALIANT CHARGER 1971 — 122
CHRYSLER VALIANT CHARGER R/T 1971 — 123
CHRYSLER VALIANT VJ 1973 — 133
CHRYSLER VALIANT VK 1975 — 143
CHRYSLER VALIANT CL 1976 — 147
CHRYSLER VALIANT CM 1978 — 155
CHRYSLER VIP 1969 — 108

CLEMENTS 1905 — 33
COTTON 1909 — 40
COTTON 1914 — 44
CRAINE 1908 — 40

DATSUN 200B 1977 — 149
DATSUN BLUEBIRD 1981 — 163

DAVIS 1902 — 23
DAY 1906 — 37
DIECASTER 1944 — 63

EARNSHAW 1905 — 33
ECO 1922 — 53
EDITH 1955 — 68
EGAN 1935 — 61
EKINS 1916 — 46

FINLAYSON 1900 — 20

FORD CORTINA TC 'SIX' 1972 — 131
FORD FAIRLANE 1967 — 100
FORD FAIRLANE ZF 1972 — 132
FORD FAIRLANE ZH 1976 — 144
FORD FAIRLANE ZJ 1979 — 158
FORD FALCON XK 1960 — 79
FORD FALCON XL 1962 — 86
FORD FALCON XM 1964 — 90
FORD FALCON XP 1965 — 93
FORD FALCON XR 1966 — 98
FORD FALCON XT 1968 — 103
FORD FALCON XW 1969 — 110
FORD FALCON XY 1970 — 118
FORD FALCON XY GT-HO PH. 3 1971 — 125
FORD FALCON XA 1972 — 129
FORD FALCON XB 1973 — 136
FORD FALCON XC 1976 — 146
FORD FALCON XC COBRA 1978 — 153
FORD FALCON XD 1979 — 156
FORD FALCON XE 1982 — 166
FORD FALCON XF 1984 — 177
FORD FALCON 'XF½' 1986 — 186
FORD LANDAU 1973 — 135
FORD LASER TURBO 1985 — 180
FORD LTD 1973 — see LANDAU 1973 — 135
FORD MODEL T ('GEELONG') 1926 — 56

FLOOD SEDAN 1904 — 31

GILGEN 1880 — 12
GMA CHEVROLET (HOLDEN BODY) 1929 — 57

GM-H HOLDEN 48-215 1948 — 64
GM-H HOLDEN FJ 1953 — 67
GM-H HOLDEN FE 1956 — 70
GM-H HOLDEN FC 1958 — 74
GM-H HOLDEN FB 1960 — 78
GM-H HOLDEN EK 1961 — 81
GM-H HOLDEN EJ 1962 — 83
GM-H HOLDEN EH 1963 — 89

GM-H HOLDEN HD 1965 — 92
GM-H HOLDEN HR 1966 — 97
GM-H HOLDEN HK 1968 — 102
GM-H HOLDEN MONARO GTS 1969 — 104
GM-H HOLDEN HT 1969 — 107
GM-H HOLDEN HG 1970 — 113
GM-H HOLDEN HQ 1971 — 120
GM-H HOLDEN HJ 1974 — 138
GM-H HOLDEN HX 1976 — 145
GM-H HOLDEN HZ 1977 — 150
GM-H HOLDEN CAMIRA JB 1982 — 168
GM-H HOLDEN CAMIRA JD 1984 — 178
GM-H HOLDEN COMMODORE VB 1978 — 154
GM-H HOLDEN COMMODORE VC 1980 — 159
GM-H HOLDEN COMMODORE VH 1981 — 164
GM-H HOLDEN COMMODORE VK 1984 — 173
GM-H HOLDEN COMMODORE VL 1986 — 181
GM-H HOLDEN GEMINI ZZ/Z 1983 — 170
GM-H HOLDEN SUNBIRD UC 1978 — 152
GM-H HOLDEN TORANA LC 1969/70 — 114
GM-H HOLDEN TORANA GTR-X 1970 — 117
GM-H HOLDEN TORANA LJ 1972 — 128
GM-H HOLDEN TORANA LH 1974 — 137
GM-H HOLDEN TORANA LX 1977 — 148
GM-H STATESMAN 1971 — 121
GM-H STATESMAN WB 1980 — 162

GOGGOMOBIL DART 1958 — 75
GRAYSON 1906 — 37
GVANG 1972 — 130

HAINES & GRUT 1908 — 39
HAMMER 1900 — 22
HARTNETT 1949 — 65
HDT COMMODORE 1980 — 161
HIGHLAND 1897 — 15
HOLDEN (STEAMCAR) 1911 — 41
HUMBLE 1904 — 31
HUNTER 1969 — 105
HUSBAND 1910 — 40

ILINGA AF2 1975 — 140
INNES 1903 — 27

JB MINOR 1949 — 66
JESSOP 1906 — 35

KNIGHT-EATON 1893 — 12
KNOWLES 1903 — 26

LEAN 1901 — 22
LEWIS 1900 — 21
LEYLAND P76 1973 — 134
LEYLAND FORCE 7 1974 — 139
LINCOLN 1919 — 49
LLOYD-HARTNETT 1957 — 72

MACQUE 1913 — 43
McDONALD 1905 — 33
McINTOSH 1893 — 12
MARKS-MOIR 1923 — 54
MARRIOTT 1903 — 29
MAYMAN 1904 — 32
MCM 1945 — 63
MINI MOKE 1966 — 95
MITSUBISHI SIGMA GJ 1982 — 167
MITSUBISHI COLT RB 1982 — 165
MITSUBISHI MAGNA 1985 — 179
MODISTACH QUAD 1903 — 28
MORRIS MINI K 1969 — 111
MORRIS MARSHALL 1957 — 71
MORRIS 1500 NOMAD 1969 — 109

NIELSEN 1904 — 32
NISSAN PULSAR TURBO ET 1984 — 174
NISSAN PINTARA 1986 — 183
NISSAN SKYLINE 1986 — 185
NORMAN 1907 — 38
NOTA TYPE 4 1971 — 124

OHLYMEYER 'JIGGER' 1904 — 30

PALM 1917 — 47
PENDER-HERTEL 1897 — 16
PERENTTI 1983 — 172
PHIZAKERLEY 1902 — 24
PIONEER 1897 — 14
PRITCHARD 1975 — 142
PUCKRIDGE 1903 — 25
PURVIS EUREKA 1977 — 151

REVILLE 1950 — 66
'RICHARDS' CHRYSLER 1936 — 62
RICHTER 1903 — 28
ROO 1917 — 47
ROSSITER 1908 — 40

SHEARER 1896 — 13
SHIELS 1933 — 60

SOUTHERN SIX 1922 — 54
SOUTHERN CROSS 1933 — 59
SPANMORE LTD 1980 — 160
SULMAN-SIMPLEX 1923 — 55
SUMMIT 1922 — 52
SUTTON 1899 — 19
SWINNERTON 1907 — 38
SWINNERTON 1915 — 45
SYME 1906 — 36

TAIPAN 1986 — 188
TARRANT 1905 — 34
TAYLOR 1906 — 35
TD 2000 1986 — 184
THOMSON 1898 — 17
TILBROOKS 1953 — 68
TILL 1906 — 35
TILLI CAPTON 1957 — 71
TONTALA 1955 — 68
TOY 1905 — 35
TOYOTA CORONA 1983 — 171
TOYOTA COROLLA TWIN CAM 1986 — 182
TRACKSON 1901 — 23
TRESCOWTHICK 'QUAD' 1903 — 29
TREVETHAN 1901 — 23
TRIAD 1984 — 176
TURNBULL 1914 — 44
TUTTLE 1916 — 46

VICHIE 1920 — 50
VOLKSWAGEN 'CLAYTON' BEETLE 1961 — 80
VOLKSWAGEN COUNTRY BUGGY 1967 — 99

WASP 1984 — 175
WEGE 1921 — 51
WILES 1949 — 66

ZETA SALOON 1963 — 87
ZETA SPORTS 1964 — 91
ZIEGLER 1898 — 18

ACKNOWLEGMENTS

Naturally, a work such as *Aussie Cars* requires detailed research and considerable trouble has been taken to ensure accuracy by corroborating information from as many sources as possible.

Most of the details relating to cars prior to 1948 came from information collected by Pedr Davis, in the form of original documents, photographs, newspaper reports and transcripts of interviews with pioneer car makers. This was expanded by research in museums and public libraries and with information passed on by such people as Frank Wetton, Max Stahl, Ian Debenham, Martin Hallett and Bill Sidebottom.

The work of other writers on the subject of early Australian motoring, most notably Terry and Maree Gilltrap and Max Gregory, was referred to.

Details on cars built after 1948 was culled from my own observations and with the help of car company files, Automotive News Service files, press releases, original specification sheets, workshop manuals and publications by Automated Data Services (*The Red Book* etc). I also pored over articles and road tests published in Australian car magazines including *Modern Motor*, *Wheels*, *Car Australia* (formerly *Motor Manual*), *Racing Car News* and the 'late' *Sports Car World*.

**Tony Davis,
January 1987.**

THE LAST WORD

Is there something we've missed?

Is there a little-known Aussie car that you have information about, or photos of? We would be very happy to receive details for future editions of this book.

We have plans to follow *Aussie Cars* with a companion volume called *Aussie Cars – The Specials*.

In this we will cover the enormous number of brilliant 'one-offs', racing cars, experimental cars and novelty vehicles built downunder.

We have already started the research and have unearthed a large number of likely inclusions.

If you own, have built, or know of an eligible vehicle, please send us a photo and relevant information. If all goes well, we should be able to preserve the memory for posterity.

Please write to P.O. Box 203, Hurstville, NSW 2220.□